WALKS & TOURS
DUBROVNIK

YOUR TAILOR-MADE TRIP
STARTS HERE

Tailor-made trips and unique adventures crafted by local experts

Rough Guides has been inspiring travellers with lively and thought-provoking guidebooks for more than 35 years. Now we're linking you up with selected local experts to craft your dream trip. They will put together your perfect itinerary and book it at local rates.

Don't follow the crowd – find your own path.

HOW ROUGHGUIDES.COM/TRIPS WORKS

STEP 1

Pick your dream destination, tell us what you want and submit an enquiry.

STEP 2

Fill in a short form to tell your local expert about your dream trip and preferences.

STEP 3

Our local expert will craft your tailor-made itinerary. You'll be able to tweak and refine it until you're completely satisfied.

STEP 4

Book online with ease, pack your bags and enjoy the trip! Our local expert will be on hand 24/7 while you're on the road.

BENEFITS OF PLANNING AND BOOKING AT ROUGHGUIDES.COM/TRIPS

PLAN YOUR ADVENTURE WITH LOCAL EXPERTS
Rough Guides' English-speaking local experts are hand-picked, based on their experience in the travel industry and their impeccable standards of customer service.

SAVE TIME AND GET ACCESS TO LOCAL KNOWLEDGE
When a local expert plans your trip, you save time and money when you book, even during high season. You won't be charged for using a credit card either.

MAKE TRAVEL A BREEZE: BOOK WITH PEACE OF MIND
Enjoy stress-free travel when you use Rough Guides' secure online booking platform. All bookings come with a money-back guarantee.

WHAT DO OTHER TRAVELLERS THINK ABOUT ROUGH GUIDES TRIPS?

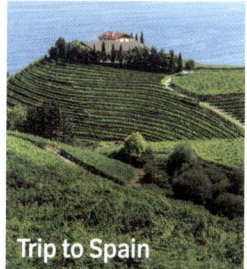
Trip to Spain

This Spain tour company did a fantastic job to make our dream trip perfect. We gave them our travel budget, told them where we would like to go, and they did all of the planning. Our drivers and tour guides were always on time and very knowledgable. The hotel accommodations were better than we would have found on our own. Only one time did we end up in a location that we had not intended to be in. We called the 24 hour phone number, and they immediately fixed the situation.

Don A, USA

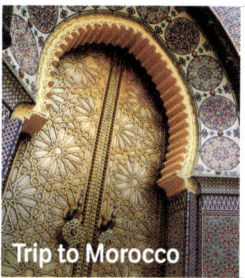
Trip to Morocco

Our trip was fantastic! Transportation, accommodations, guides – all were well chosen! The hotels were well situated, well appointed and had helpful, friendly staff. All of the guides we had were very knowledgeable, patient, and flexible with our varied interests in the different sites. We particularly enjoyed the side trip to Tangier! Well done! The itinerary you arranged for us allowed maximum coverage of the country with time in each city for seeing the important places.

Sharon, USA

PLAN AND BOOK YOUR TRIP AT ROUGHGUIDES.COM/TRIPS

CONTENTS

Introduction

Best walks & tours for.. 6
Discover Dubrovnik..10
Food and drink..16
Shopping 20
Entertainment...22
Outdoor activities...24
Chronology..26

Trip plans

Walk 1: Around the City Walls 30
Walk 2: Stradun and Old Townhighlights............................. 36
Walk 3: Around Prijeko and south of Stradun 43
Walk 4: Outside the Ploče Gate... 49
Tour 5: Lapad, Babin Kuk and Gruž 53
Tour 6: Lokrum Island 58
Tour 7: The Elaphite Islands 61
Tour 8: Mljet.. 66
Tour 9: Cavtat 71
Tour 10: Trsteno and Ston 75
Walk 11: Korčula 79

Directory

Accommodation 86
Restaurants.. 94
Nightlife 104
Essentials... 106
Language 116
Books and film.. 120
About this book 122
Credits... 123
Index.. 124

Back to nature
Revel in the greenery of the National Park in Mljet (tour 8) where you can hire a bike. Lokrum's trails lead through lush botanical gardens and a saltwater lagoon (tour 6).

Best walks & tours for...

Best views
A walk around the City Walls (walk 1) is a must. Take the cable car to Mount Srđ (walk 4) for sweeping views. Head out to Lapad (tour 5) for glimpses of the Elaphite Islands.

Escaping the crowds
Hop on a boat or take the bus to pretty Cavtat (tour 9) for a walk around the peninsula. Take a short drive to Zaton (tour 10) on the way to Trsteno for a waterside lunch.

Foodies
Head out to Mali Ston (tour 10) for what are regarded as the best oysters in Croatia. Spend a day in Korčula (walk 11) and sample some of the region's top wines.

History buffs
Breathtaking and beautifully preserved Renaissance architecture surrounds you on a wander through the Old Town (walk 2). Hike up to Fort Lovrijenac after exploring the historic City Walls (walk 1).

Island hopping
Choose from a short jaunt to Lokrum (tour 6) or a longer trip to the Elaphite Islands (tour 7) or Mljet (tour 8). If you want to go further afield, spend the night in Korčula (walk 11).

Seaside fun
Clamber among the rocks and pebbly beaches of Lapad and Babin Kuk (tour 5). Banje (walk 4) is the city's beach, with great views of the old port.

Street life
Join the strollers along the main Stradun thoroughfare (walk 2) and take in the lively atmosphere of the tiny bars squeezed into the narrow lanes leading up to Prijeko (walk 3).

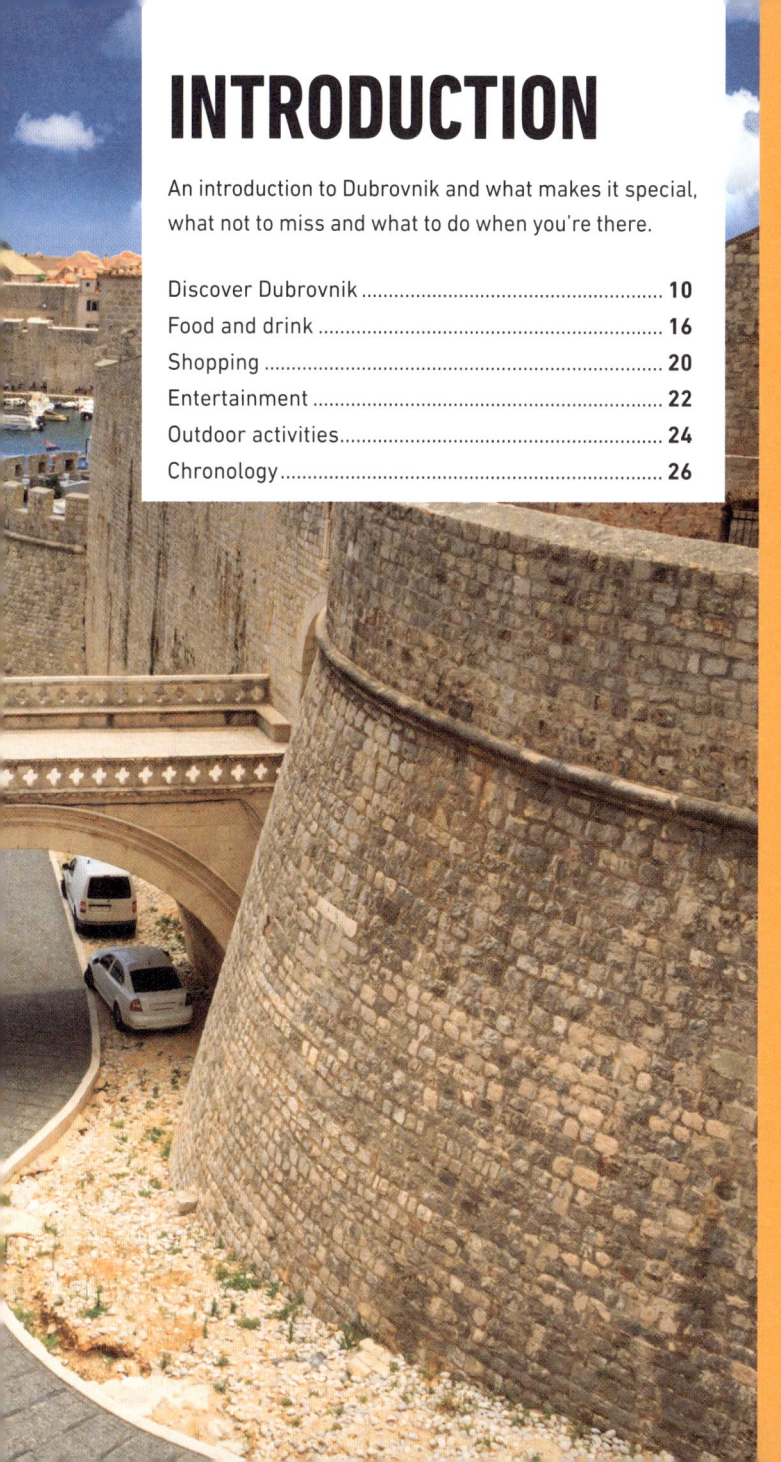

INTRODUCTION

An introduction to Dubrovnik and what makes it special, what not to miss and what to do when you're there.

Discover Dubrovnik **10**
Food and drink **16**
Shopping **20**
Entertainment **22**
Outdoor activities **24**
Chronology **26**

Discover Dubrovnik

Behind the fairy-tale façade of Dubrovnik's medieval walls lies a city of inexhaustible beauty. It's as beguiling now as when Lord Byron clapped eyes on it two centuries ago and called it the 'Pearl of the Adriatic'.

Framed by the deep blue waters of the Adriatic Sea, the former Republic of Ragusa enjoys one of the most dramatic settings along Croatia's Dalmatian coast. Dubrovnik was once a powerful maritime trading port, and this UNESCO World Heritage Site still shows an independent spirit born of centuries of keeping an eye on its enemies with a clever combination of diplomacy and hefty fortifications.

Within its medieval walls are shimmering marble streets lined with green-shuttered stone houses. Its two most impressive buildings – the Rector's Palace and Sponza Palace – survived the devastating earthquake of 1667 that destroyed much of its Venetian Gothic and Renaissance architecture. The remade baroque city took another battering in 1991, when Serbian and Montenegrin forces besieged Dubrovnik during the bitter Yugoslav civil war. With admirable speed, the city was repaired once again. One of the few remaining scars was the tell-tale brightness of newer terracotta roof tiles.

Nowadays, the only sieges are from large groups of cruise passengers and coach parties that throng the streets during the day. Come late afternoon, outdoor café tables hum with contented coffee drinkers happy to reclaim the city from the day-trippers. Warm summer evenings bring a magical ambience, with music drifting from classical concerts held in historic buildings. In the many outdoor restaurants, diners feast on plates of fresh seafood before they head off to the bars tucked into the narrow streets off Stradun.

Geography and layout

Dubrovnik is on Croatia's southeastern tip, just 37km (23 miles) from the border with Montenegro. A forbidding ridge of bare brown mountains flanks its northern side, a stark contrast to the vibrant blue of the Adriatic Sea. The Elaphite Islands and Mljet are to the northwest, and beyond those are the fertile vineyards and villages of the Pelješac peninsula.

Dubrovnik

Although the Old Town is the major focus for most visitors, it occupies a small portion of the city. The area of Ploče, where grand hotels overlook the coast, is to the east. The workaday port of Gruž hugs the coast to the west, and

Pearl of the Adriatic

the Lapad and Babin Kuk peninsulas hive off southwards. The latter two are where many of the family-oriented hotels are based, as they're close to the main beaches. Gruž, Lapad and Babin Kuk are all connected to the Old Town by an efficient network of buses. Boats make regular 15-minute trips from the Old Town's harbour to the tiny island of Lokrum, which manages to squeeze in a monastery, saltwater lake, botanical gardens and rocky beaches.

Day trips from Dubrovnik

Dubrovnik makes a good base for visiting the nearby islands and villages. Regular ferries and catamarans leave from Gruž harbour to the island of Mljet and the Elaphite archipelago of Lopud, Šipan and Koločep. Further afield is the island of Korčula, which can be combined with a road trip to Mali Ston on the Pelješac peninsula to sample the village's renowned oysters.

South of Dubrovnik is the village of Cavtat, which juts out on a peninsula that can be reached by boat or by bus. This is part of the Konavle region, the last Croatian one before Montenegro, and home to vineyards and numerous bicycle trails through hills and valleys.

Beyond Dubrovnik

There's no shortage of tour companies in Dubrovnik offering day excursions to its two foreign neighbours. Mostar in Bosnia-Herzegovina is about a two-hour drive away, and it's an even shorter journey to Kotor in Montenegro. Buses to Split further north along the Adriatic coast take about four hours, and the Pelješac bridge that opened in 2022 makes the journey even easier.

History

For such a tiny place, Dubrovnik has a fascinating history. There were signs of a settlement as early as the sixth century. Over the centuries it was taken over by the Byzantines, the Venetians, the Hungarians and the French. The first recorded mention of the Republic of Ragusa was in 1181; by the sixteenth century, the city had a powerful merchant navy with more than 200 vessels that traded all over the known world. It started to decline in the seventeenth century when the English and the Dutch grew in strength, and the republic was finally dissolved in 1808 when Napoleon invaded.

When Yugoslavia started to disintegrate and war broke out between Serbs and Croats, Dubrovnik was besieged in October 1991. The port at Gruž and the airport were destroyed, and the Old Town subjected to mortar attack. Almost 100 civilians were killed in Dubrovnik and numerous buildings damaged, but major reconstruction restored the city.

Art and architecture

The fifteenth and sixteenth centuries were a prosperous time, when the

Republic flourished both commercially and artistically. Although the Dubrovnik School is not widely known outside Croatia, its artists produced a sound body of work. Much of their output was destroyed in the fire that followed the earthquake of 1667, but some can still be seen. Three works by Nikola Božidarević (1464–1517) are in the Dominican Monastery Museum, which also displays a richly textured *Baptism of Christ*, by Lovro Dobričević (1420–78); his portrait of St Blaise is in the Franciscan Monastery and a polyptych in the Dance church. Another *Baptism of Christ*, this one by Mihajlo Hamzić (died *c*.1518), can be found in the Rector's Palace.

Architecture also blossomed during the Italian Renaissance, spearheaded by the Florentine Michelozzo Michelozzi; it was in the fifteenth century that some of the city's most splendid buildings were built or embellished. Most were destroyed by the earthquake, and what didn't survive was rebuilt in the baroque style that now dominates the Old Town.

Climate

Average temperatures in winter (November–February) range from 8–12°C (46–54°F), April, May and October 14–18°C (57–65°F), June and September 21–22°C (70–72°F), July and August 24–25°C (75–77°F), although summer highs can soar beyond 30°C (86°F). The best times to visit Dubrovnik are May to June and September to October. The weather should be fine and sunny and the sea is usually still warm in the autumn. The town will be less crowded, accommodation easier to find and flights cheaper. Dubrovnik can be lovely on a crisp, cold winter day, especially during the Christmas market in December and the Dubrovnik Winter Festival. But there are wet and windy days too, and flight schedules taper off during the winter. Many restaurants and hotels close, and fewer boats run to the islands.

Population

The population of Dubrovnik is about 42,000. The vast majority are Croats, with small groups of Muslims and Serbs as well as a tiny Jewish population. Over recent years, there has been an increase of people with Croatian backgrounds who have emigrated to the city to run businesses. There has also been a return of residents who had left Dubrovnik during the conflict of the early 1990s.

People and customs

Dalmatians often resemble their Italian neighbours across the Adriatic, mainly in their manners and attitudes towards fashion: they do like to be smartly dressed. They even do their own version of the Italian *passeggiata* called the *džir*, when people signal the end of a working day by strolling leisurely down the main pedestrianised street

Ornate detail on Onofrio fountain

Don't leave Dubrovnik without...

Walking the City Walls. Get a glimpse of daily life in the Old Town and absorb the city's history by walking around these magnificent medieval fortifications. See page 30.

Having a sundowner at Buža Bar. Watch the sun go down from this simple little bar that clings to the side of the cliff below the City Walls. Look out for the sign that says 'Cold drinks with the most beautiful view'. That's exactly what you get – plastic cups and all. See page 47.

Going up to Mount Srd. Some of best views not only of the city but also the surrounding countryside and the coastline can be seen from the top of this mountain looming over Dubrovnik. You can ride the cable car, take an hour-long hike or combine the two. See page 52.

Eating the 'world's best oysters'. Back in 1936, the oysters from the nearby village of Mali Ston were given this accolade at the General Trades International Exhibition in London. Hyperbole or not, the oysters certainly are delicious and can be found on many menus in Dubrovnik as well as in Ston on the Pelješac peninsula. See page 78.

Discovering recent history. The excellent War Photo Limited gallery has a permanent exhibition of photographs covering the Balkans conflict as well as temporary displays of compelling war photography from around the world. See page 45.

Escaping the city for a day. Take the 15-minute ferry from the Old Port to the small island of Lokrum, where you can wander through wooded trails and botanical gardens, take a dip in a saltwater lagoon or go swimming off the rocks. See page 58.

Watching the sunset from Park Orsula. Just south of the city is an amphitheatre that's become the venue for the Orsuladanja summer music festival. But you don't need to be there for the festival to catch breathtaking views of the sun setting over the Old Port. See page 23.

Stradun, stopping for a coffee and – most importantly – people-watching.

Unlike their Italian neighbours, however, shopkeepers and restaurateurs in Dubrovnik tend to keep their businesses open throughout the day. Most museums are closed on Monday, with a few closed on Tuesday instead, but the City Walls are open every day.

Religion

Croatia is an overwhelmingly Roman Catholic country, and church attendance soared immediately after independence in 1991. It has tailed off considerably since then, although there is still a great deal of enthusiasm for the many religious festivals held throughout the year.

Ferry shuttling between the Pelješac peninsula and Korčula

Festive February

You can't be in Dubrovnik for long without realising that St Blaise (Sveti Vlaho) is the city's patron saint. Not only does his image appear over the Pile and Ploče Gates flanking the Old Town, but he also has his own church and his relics are kept in the Cathedral Treasury. This Armenian bishop, who was martyred in the third century, is celebrated in exuberant style in early February, bringing cheer to an otherwise gloomy month. Two days of festivities attract thousands of people to the streets of the Old Town to watch the colourful processions. Flags and banners cover the buildings, and national costumes are dusted off as everyone joins in the two days of music, dancing and feasting.

The party doesn't end there. Depending on when Easter falls, the pre-Lenten carnival usually takes place at some point in February. Cue more music, dancing and general merry-making.

Tourism

Tourism is the mainstay of the local economy, and increases every year. However, the relentless rise of the cruise industry and package coach tours means that the city is quite overwhelmed for much of the day during the summer.

The standard of English spoken by people in the tourism industry is very high, particularly among younger people. But people of all ages switch easily between the main languages being spoken by tourists in Dubrovnik, namely English, Italian and German.

Politics and economics

Since Croatia joined the European Union in 2013, its economy has been shrinking as it has been unable to generate much business outside of the tourism industry. Its expensive, bulky and bureaucracy-laden public sector continues to drain money from the economy, something that the government has been very slow to rectify.

Croatia's current head of government is Prime Minister Andrej Plenković, who is the leader of the conservative centre-right Croatian Democratic Union (HDZ). The current head of state is President Zoran Milanović. Mayor of Dubrovnik until 2017, left-of-centre Andro Vlahušić voiced his concerns about the fact that his city was too expensive for locals to live in. During his tenure he devised various programmes to entice young graduates to return to the city once they had finished their studies elsewhere. His successor, Mato Franković of the HDZ party, made the radical decision to drastically cut the daily number of tourists allowed inside the City Walls to 8,000 people. In January 2023, Croatia joined the eurozone and the Schengen Area, which inevitably resulted in rising prices.

Dubrovnik viewed from above

Top tips for exploring Dubrovnik

Stradun in season. In the height of summer, when as many as six cruise ships have disgorged their passengers, Stradun can become a barely moving sea of people. This is the time for you to explore quieter parts of the city or one of the islands. The cruise crowds will have left by about 4pm, so that's the time to have a more leisurely stroll and stop for a coffee.

Dubrovnik Pass. If you're there for more than a day and plan to do some sightseeing, the Dubrovnik Pass will pay for itself very quickly. The tourist pass includes entry to most attractions – including the City Walls – as well as free buses and restaurant discounts.

Gruž market. Dubrovnik's biggest and most authentic food market takes place every morning near the Jadrolinja ferry port. It's a lively affair, full of residents stocking up on fresh produce. There's a smaller daily market in Gundulić Square in the Old Town, which, after locals do their shopping first thing in the morning, becomes more of a tourist attraction.

Bring swimming shoes. Although there are sandy beaches on some of the nearby islands, the ones in Dubrovnik are either pebbly or rocky. If your feet are sensitive, you're better off wearing protective shoes. You can find these easily in local beach shops if you don't bring your own.

Get to know the islands. It's very easy to take boats, ferries and catamarans to nearby islands including Mljet, the Elaphite archipelago and Korčula, although crossings tend to peter out from November to March. Some of the islands, notably Korčula, are worth an overnight stay.

Arriving from the airport. The airport transfer is straightforward, efficient and very cheap. A single fare is about a tenth the price of a taxi, which wouldn't be allowed into the car-free Old Town anyway. Buses are timed to coincide with each flight and will drop you off outside the Pile Gate.

Get lost and look up. The Old Town is packed with narrow streets, many of which lead up and down stairs to hidden flower-filled courtyards and into tiny stone arcades. It's a delight just to wander and explore, and especially to look up and spot one fascinating architectural detail after another.

Summer Festival. At the height of the season for about six weeks in July and August, the Summer Festival fills the streets of the Old Town night after night after the daily tourists have gone home. It does get extremely busy, and you have to book accommodation well in advance, but it is an incredible spectacle.

Korčula Town is only a hop away

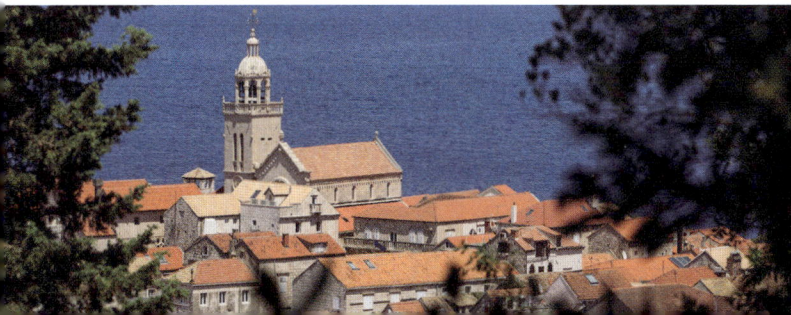

Food and drink

For a relatively small city, Dubrovnik has an enviable range of restaurants offering a mouth-watering selection of fresh fish, seafood and succulent meats. And within its narrow streets are a few culinary surprises.

The growth of the cruise industry in Dubrovnik has brought with it higher prices than you'll find in most parts of Croatia, and some of the more touristy places take advantage of the fact that they're unlikely to see these customers again. But this same influx has prompted many restaurateurs to up their game and devise more creative dishes. You're likely to find a stronger international flavour mingling with traditional Dalmatian cuisine – for example, with more Asian influences being adapted successfully.

Local cuisine

The Italian influence is unmistakable in Dubrovnik's cuisine, which features an almost dizzying array of pasta and risotto dishes. But seafood is the star, which you'll find in most restaurants – even some pizzerias. The word for fish is *riba*, and varieties range from gilthead bream *(orada)*, red mullet *(trilja)* and sea bream *(arbun)* to the humbler mackerel *(skuše)*, sardines *(srdele)* and anchovies *(inćuni)*, all excellent when simply grilled and served with a salad.

Seafood

Prevalent on Dubrovnik's menus is shellfish *(školjke)*, including mussels, which rather confusingly are known both as *mušule* and *dagnje*, shrimps *(račiće)* and Dublin Bay prawns *(škampi)*. You will often see *mušule na buzaru* or *bouzara*, which means the molluscs are cooked with wine, parsley, garlic (lots) and breadcrumbs; some versions also include tomatoes. Squid *(lignji)* and octopus *(hobotnica)* also appear on most menus, cooked in a variety of ways: fried *(prigani* or *pržene)*, grilled *(na žaru)* or stuffed *(punjeni)*. One of the most popular dishes is a simple octopus salad with garlic and olive oil.

On more upmarket menus you may find lobster *(jastog)* or oysters *(oštrige)*: the former is more prevalent on the island of Mljet, the latter up the coast in Ston and Mali Ston, where the best oysters are farmed.

Meat

Meat lovers should not despair. As well as the tasty Dalmatian smoked ham *(dalmatinski pršut)*, similar to prosciutto, that appears as a first course on most menus, there is usually chicken breast *(pileća prsa)* or chicken escalope *(pileći file)* and pork cutlets *(svinjski kutlet)*, along

Lobster pasta

with steak (simply called *biftek*) and platters of grilled meats.

On some of the nearby islands, restaurants specialise in cooking meat *ispod peke* – under a cast-iron bell surrounded by hot ashes, so the food cooks slowly and all the juices are retained. This iron bell is also used to make the Dubrovnik stew known as *zelena menestra*, a hearty dish of slow-cooked smoked ham, sausages, cabbage and potatoes.

Vegetables

Vegetarians are not too well catered for, although the salads are usually fresh and ample; salad with feta cheese *(sirom)* is especially popular, and pasta with a non-meat, tomato-based sauce is usually available. Fresh vegetables *(svježe povrće)* are seasonal (which shows they are both fresh and local), and may include courgettes, aubergines and the ubiquitous Swiss chard *(blitve)*. Polenta is a common accompaniment to dishes. You can often get crêpes *(palačinke)*, either savoury or sweet. And, of course, there is always pizza, which is usually very good indeed and often comes in eye-poppingly generous portions. But if you want some innovative dishes, try the Old Town's only exclusively vegan restaurant, Nishta (see page 96), located just north of Stradun.

Pasta and risotto

Pasta is ubiquitous on menus. Plates of tagliatelle and spaghetti will have the usual tomato-based sauces, but many will also have seafood such as prawns and scampi. Look out for Dubrovnik speciality *šporki makaruli*, a rich pasta dish of slow-cooked beef. And then there's the Istrian flavour of truffle sauces added to noodles. Risotto (*rižot* or *rižoto*) is just as common: *rižot plodovi mora* is a mixed seafood risotto, and *crni rižoto* (black risotto) is made with squid or cuttlefish, the rice blackened by the ink.

Cheeses

Influences from northern Croatia can be found here, including Istrian cow's milk cheese infused with truffles and the hard sheep's milk cheese from Pag known as *paški sir*. Dubrovnik has its own version of the latter, which is made into small rounds and preserved in olive oil.

Sweets

Although Croatians have a sweet tooth, judging by the extremely sticky, creamy cakes on sale in pastry shops *(slastičarnice)* and cafés, these are eaten as snacks, usually with coffee. Local people don't go in for puddings in a big way. You are most likely to be offered ice cream *(sladoled)*, fresh fruit *(voće)*, baklava and *dubrovačka rožata*, the local version of crème caramel, which can be excellent.

The menu

Lunch *(ručak)* and dinner *(večera)* will generally have the same menu.

The popular octopus salad

Seafood platter

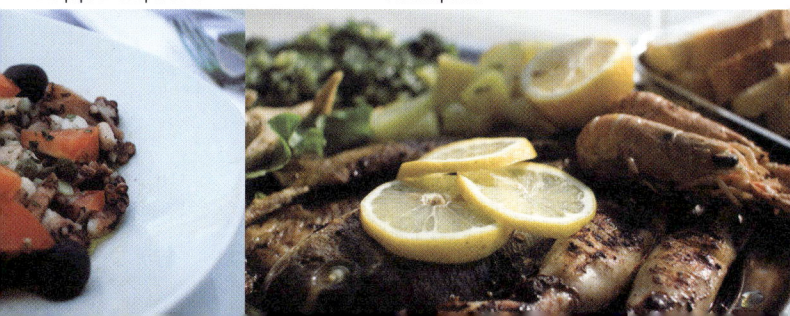

Sweet treats

Peer into the windows of pastry and souvenir shops and you'll see a selection of Dubrovnik delicacies prettily wrapped up. A favourite is *arancini*, which has nothing to do with the Sicilian rice-ball snack but is instead candied orange peel. It's often sold with bags of caramelised almonds (*bruštulane mjendule*), which are offered as nibbles in bars. You'll also see *kotonjata* and *mantala*, which sometimes resemble Turkish delight. The former are cubes of quince (often translated as quince cheese, although there's nothing cheesy about it) and the latter are made from grape must. *Kotonjata* is also poured into moulds to make desserts.

Cold starters usually include a Dalmatian platter with *pršut* (like prosciutto), cheese and olives, as well as soups, octopus salad and marinated anchovies. Warm starters include pasta and risotto dishes, most of which are big enough to suffice as a main course. Grilled meats, skewered fish and seafood platters are common main courses, as are whole grilled fish. As fresh fish is often charged by the kilo, agree the price beforehand to save any unpleasant surprises when it comes to paying the bill.

Where to eat

Alfresco dining dominates, adding a relaxed sense of informality even during chillier months when heaters are brought outside. Even the restaurants in the Old Town that are tucked away in narrow streets usually find space to plant tables outside. High-end restaurants in historic locations, such as Restaurant 360° (closed in winter) above the Old Port, will have prices to match. Prijeko in the Old Town, which runs parallel to Stradun, is one long street of restaurants, but most are of very average quality. A few honourable exceptions include Stara Loza (see page 97), Rozario (see page 97) and the vegan restaurant Nishta (see page 96).

Snacks

A typical bakery (*pekara*) will have savoury filo pastry pies known as *burek* and sweet pastries, with the latter more prevalent in pastry shops (*slastičarnice*). If you want a second breakfast, the Dubrovnik version of brunch is *marenda*, which consists of usually smaller and cheaper versions of lunch dishes. The restaurants serving this aren't as plentiful as they were, so look out for lunchtime specials in some of the smaller cafés or even in a few of the bakeries.

Little hole-in-the-wall pizza takeaways will sell pizza by the slice. Wine bars in the Old Town often serve plates of cheese and

Table with a view

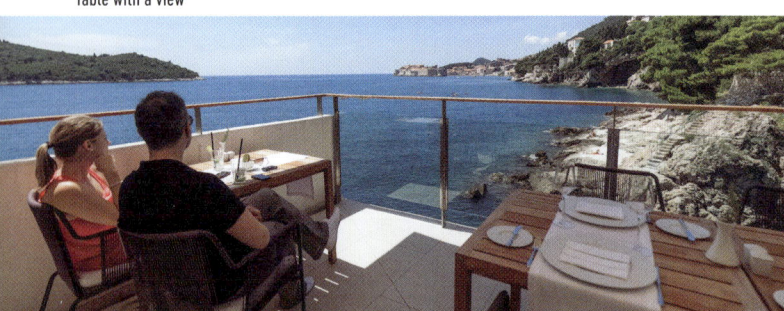

> **Food and drink prices**
>
> Approximate prices are based on a two-course meal for one, with a glass of house wine.
> € = under €35
> €€ = €35–60
> €€€ = over €60

charcuterie to go with your wine, which make an appetising aperitif or even a meal in itself.

Meals

Restaurant is *restoran*, but many eating places describe themselves as a *konoba*, which used to be a kind of rustic tavern. (Originally it was a cellar used to store wine and preserved food.) It still is in some rural areas, but in the city the meaning has become blurred. Some upmarket restaurants cheerfully call themselves a *konoba*, while a humbler establishment is a *restoran*. Many cafés (often spelled *caffe* the Italian way) have full menus for lunch and dinner as well.

Drinks

The vineyards in the Pelješac peninsula just north of Dubrovnik are home to some of Croatia's top wines, but as they're rarely exported they might not be familiar to the average wine drinker. Red wine *(crno vino)* prevails in this part of the Dalmatian coast, the primary grape of which is *plavac mali*. This produces one of the best wines in the region, the full-bodied *Dingač*. *Postup* is a darker red from the same grape. White wines *(bijelo vino)* include *grk* and *pošip*, grown on the island of Korčula, and *dubrovačka malvasija*.

The local dessert wine is *prošek*, which gained notoriety when Croatia joined the European Union in 2013. EU officials assumed there would be confusion between this sweet dessert wine and prosecco, a dry sparkling wine from Italy, and ordered the Croatian producers to change the name that had been in existence for about 2,000 years. Not surprisingly, Croatia launched an appeal.

The Croatian national spirit, *rakija*, is made from distilled alcohol flavoured with fruit or herbs. There's also a version made from walnuts called *orahovac*. The recipes for it differ not only from place to place but also from distiller to distiller.

Many people drink beer *(pivo)* with meals. Croatian beer is tasty, inexpensive and not too high in alcohol. Dubrovnik's water *(voda)* is safe to drink and tastes fine, and some restaurants will offer carafes of tap water free of charge, although most prefer to sell you bottled mineral water. Coffee *(kava)* is usually strong and good. Coffee with milk is *kava s mlijekom*; if you want it black, ask for *kava* or espresso.

Korčula is known for its white wines

Shopping

Although Dubrovnik is not the place for serious shopping, there's a growing number of independent Croatian boutiques and designers to be found among the souvenir shops. And there's certainly no shortage of places to buy high-quality food.

Dubrovnik doesn't have the range of shops you would expect of such a heavily visited city, but there are few local items worth looking out for.

Markets

Dubrovnik's markets are the best places to browse and to buy fresh local produce – useful not only for those in self-catering accommodation but also for putting together a picnic or simply buying whatever is in season.

The main markets are the daily ones in Gruž harbour – where there is also a big, noisy fish market – and in Gundulić Square in the Old Town. The former is an authentically local affair, worth visiting if you can get there early, because this is when Gruž really comes to life. It's very convenient if you are about to get on a morning ferry and haven't had time for breakfast.

The Gundulić Square market also specialises in fresh produce but, being in the heart of tourist territory, has goods geared towards foreign visitors as well. You will find embroidered linen and lace, and products derived from locally grown lavender: bottles of oil, attractively wrapped soaps and pretty linen lavender bags. You will also see local honey for sale here, strings of fresh garlic, bags of nuts and little coronets of dried figs, garlanded with leaves.

Jewellery

Silver filigree is the speciality, and coral also features frequently. Dubrovnik Treasures at Celestina Medovića beside the Franciscan Monastery makes by hand original designs and will also make jewellery to your specifications at reasonable prices.

Fashion

Although the choice is not extensive, you can find contemporary fashion in Dubrovnik. The Robna Kuća Minčeta (www.minceta.hr) shopping centre near Gruž harbour has a decent number of men's and women's shops. For upmarket fashion, MaxMara has a branch in Stradun. The biggest selection of designer clothes in one space is in Maria Store (www.mariastore.hr) near the Ploče

Coral jewellery: a local speciality

Gate, featuring several dozen names including Balenciaga and Gucci.

Wine, food and lifestyle

A wide range of wines and local spirits can be found in supermarkets – some in attractive bottles, which make nice gifts. Dubrovačka Kuća in Sveti Dominika sells wine, *rakija* (brandy) and oil, and good-quality but fairly expensive souvenirs. These include embroidered cushion covers and strings of Licitar hearts – honey cakes that are dried, painted red and decorated. One of the most innovative shops in Dubrovnik, Life According to KAWA (www.kawa.life), is just outside Ploče Gate on Hvarska. Here you'll find a wide range of Croatian craft beer, local wines, olive oils, condiments and other foods from around the world. The shop also showcases original Croatian design in homeware, fashion and accessories.

Ties and hats

Ties, they say, were invented in Croatia. In the mid-seventeenth century, the cravat, a loosely tied scarf worn by Croatian soldiers, became popular in Paris when it was seen adorning the necks of Croatian mercenaries in the service of Louis XIII.

A range of high-quality pure silk ties, made by the revered Potomac Company, can be found in the Croata Museum Concept Store at Pred Dvorom 2 (near the Cathedral) and in the same company's outlet in the Hotel Excelsior.

Embroidery and lace

You will not have to look far for these items. In fact, they are hard to avoid. In the large square just outside Pile Gate, stalls offer all kinds of embroidered linen and lace, along with handmade dolls and other trinkets. In the Old Port, women sit crocheting and embroidering the goods spread out for sale: tablecloths, napkins, cushion covers, handkerchiefs, baby clothes and much more besides.

More of the same type of stalls can be found tucked beneath the archway between Luža Square and the harbour, and on the steps leading to the Dominican Monastery.

Paintings and prints

A number of small shops and galleries sell work by contemporary Croatian artists, usually at reasonable prices. In Sveti Dominika you will find interesting works in the Sebastian Art Gallery (in the old St Sebastian church). In Marojice Kaboge (running between Stradun and Od Puča), Romana Art Gallery (www.romana-milutin.com) concentrates on the work of the Dubrovnik-born artist Romana Milutin. In Lučarica, the next street along, towards St Blaise's Church, the Artur Galerija (www.arturgallery.com) is also worth a look.

Lace is a popular souvenir

Entertainment

With a few exceptions, Dubrovnik isn't known for its throbbing nightlife. Its scene is centred more on its lively cafés and bars – but it's a very different story during the Summer Festival when revellers fill the streets.

Classical music

Throughout the summer, the Dubrovnik String Quartet and the Sorkočević Quartet give classical concerts recitals in St Saviour's Church beside the Franciscan Monastery. The Dubrovnik Symphony Orchestra performs in the city's historic venues such as the Dominican Monastery, the Revelin Fortress and the Rector's Palace. Flaming torches are placed outside the venue where an event is being held.

Folk music

The Lindo Folklore Ensemble, highly esteemed throughout Croatia, performs folk dance and song on an outdoor stage in the Lazareti on summer evenings. There are also folk dance performances on Sunday morning in Luža Square and in the village of Čilipi (near the airport).

Nightlife

Head to the Ploče Gate and beyond for a trio of venues offering contrasting nights out. Culture Club Revelin (www.clubrevelin.com) attracts international DJs to its two floors of club space, plus a huge terrace. Just outside the gate is Lazareti, which puts on electronica and punk within the old quarantine houses. Next to that is Banje Beach Restaurant Lounge & Club (www.banjebeach.com), a classic beach club that keeps going till 2am, sometimes later. Elyx Night Club by the Pile Gate offers top DJs and VIP suites.

In the Old Town, the focus is on bars and cafés, including La Bodega near the Sponza Palace, D'Vino Wine Bar in Palmotićeva near the Franciscan Monastery and the cafés encircling Gundulić Square. Troubadour Jazz Brasserie lives up to its name with live jazz playing most nights in the summer.

Off the tourist trail but popular among locals is the string of bars and cafés on Ulica Iva Vojnovića in Lapad, especially Caffe Bar What's Up and Mirakul.

One of the city's emerging districts is Gruž, where certain venues have brought a trendy vibe to the neighbourhood. Dubrovnik Beer Company (www.dubrovackapivovara.hr) on Obala Ivana Pavla runs a microbrewery and taproom and hosts live concerts. Around the corner, Love Bar's (https://lovebardubrovnik.com) rooftop terrace is a lively spot for cocktails and music at sunset.

Folk dancers in full swing

Over the years, live concerts have been staged in July and August at Park Orsula, a large amphitheatre clinging to the hillside south of the city. It's an incomparable setting to watch the sun set over the port to a soundtrack of live music by regional bands. It's a five-minute drive from the city, or a half-hour walk along an ancient path through the woods.

Festivals

There are three major festivals in Dubrovnik: the celebrations for St Blaise's day in early February, the Summer Festival in July and August and the Winter Festival from November to January.

Annual events

St Blaise's day is 3 February. The festival is ceremonially opened the preceding afternoon outside St Blaise's church, and at 10am on the day a celebratory Mass is held in front of the Cathedral, followed by a procession. The town is decked with flags and banners and the whole population joins in.

The ceremony culminates in the bishop blessing them all before releasing three white doves. Festivities continue throughout the day with music, dancing and lots of food.

February is also the month for the pre-Lenten carnival, with colourful parades in Stradun and masked balls in the large hotels. Processions are also held in Cavtat.

Dubrovnik's Summer Festival, inaugurated in 1950, lasts for about six weeks from early July to late August. It is a wonderful time to be in the city, but you need to book accommodation well in advance or you will have little chance of finding a room.

Performances are staged all over the city and usually include a performance of *Hamlet* in the dramatic setting of Fort Lovrijenac. The Marin Držić Theatre puts on dramatic and musical performances, including a number by Držić himself, the city's favourite sixteenth-century playwright. Numerous concerts are held in the beautiful atrium of the Rector's Palace. Then there are the streets of the Old Town itself, where the Natural Theatre Company performs, music is played, flaming torches burn and costumed figures add to the atmosphere.

The Dubrovnik Winter Festival heralds the arrival of Christmas from late November to 6 January with concerts in Stradun, Advent markets and a giant New Year's Eve party.

Other events include the Dubrovnik Film Festival and the Dubrovnik Good Food Festival in October and Cavtat's Summer Festival in July and August, with music and water polo. On 29 July, St Theodore's Day in Korčula is celebrated with the Moreška Sword Dance Festival. This colourful ritual – essentially a mock battle between good and evil – draws large crowds as brass bands play the battle march.

Trendy Banje Beach club

Outdoor activities

This part of the Adriatic coast has many ways to tempt outdoorsy types as well as swimmers keen to explore the clear blue waters. Learn to dive or take to the hills on a hike or bike ride.

Although Dubrovnik is principally a city destination, there are a number of sports and outdoor activities on offer. Most are on the water, but others take advantage of the rugged and dramatic landscapes throughout the region.

Swimming

Dubrovnik's main beach, Banje, is a pebbly one just beyond the Ploče Gate, where you can also water-ski. It's mainly public although part of it is sectioned off for one of the beach bars. About 1.5km (0.9 miles) further south is a stretch of shingle, pebbles and a small bit of sand at Sveti Jakov past the Villa Dubrovnik hotel. On the western side of the old town is a rocky beach at the Dance promontory. There are also rocky beaches accessible from the Buža Bar that clings to the cliff beneath Dubrovnik's City Walls.

The pebbly beach in Lapad Bay has a full range of facilities for families, as does the large pebbly Copacabana beach on the Babin Kuk peninsula. Copacabana also has facilities for people with disabilities.

Take the little ferry to Lokrum and choose from the shallow saltwater lake and the rocky and shingle beaches on the southern side where's there also a naturist beach.

Your best bet for sandy beaches would be to head to Šunj on Lopud and Saplunara beach on Mljet.

Diving

A vibrant underwater world can be explored on diving trips with Blue Planet (www.blueplanet-diving.com), based at the Hotel Dubrovnik Palace in Lapad, and Abyss (www.dubrovnik diving.com). Choose from beginner PADI courses to half-day, full-day and night dives among shipwrecks and in subterranean caves.

Boating

Sea kayaking, rafting, stand-up paddleboarding and canoeing are popular and easy to arrange. Sea kayaking in the bay between Fort Bokar and Fort Lovrijenac (just outside the City Walls) is run by Adventure Dalmatia (www.adventure dalmatia.com). Kayaking around Lokrum Island (with transfers from the city) is organised by Adria Adventure (www.kayakingcroaitia.com) and Adriatic Kayak Tours (www.adriatickayaktours.com), which

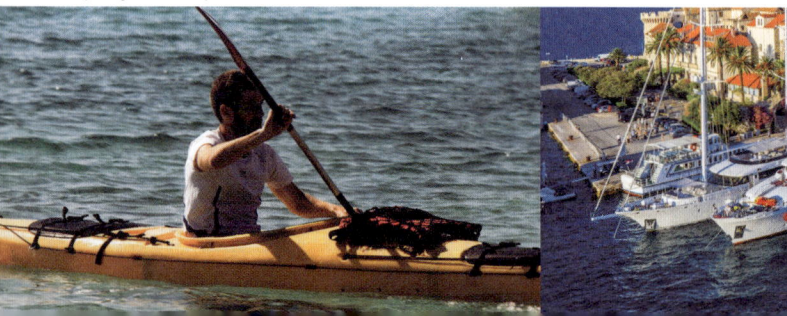

Kayaking near the City Walls

also offers kayaking from Lopud to Šipan and cycling around Šipan.

Get a taste of sailing by renting a sailboat with a skipper who can give you a personalised tour of the waters around Dubrovnik and the islands. Adventure Dubrovnik (www.adventuredubrovnik.com) has three-hour tours on small boats.

Cycling

Cycling is becoming more popular in the region, particularly along the Konavle coast starting at Cavtat. Adventure Dubrovnik rents high-quality bicycles in Cavtat for a minimum of three days.

If you take a day trip to Mljet, hire a bicycle at Polače harbour to make the most of the wooded trails winding through the island's national park.

Walking

Rather than take the cable car, join a guided walk up to Mount Srđ with Adventure Dalmatia (www.adventure dalmatia.com), which includes a visit to the Museum of the Homeland War. Adventure Dubrovnik (www.adventure dubrovnik.com) runs a similar excursion which is timed to catch the sunset over the city. If you want to take on the route yourself, it's very well signposted from Jadranka Cesta. You can combine walking with a gourmet picnic with Piknik Dubrovnik (www.piknik dubrovnik.com), which offers self-guided or escorted hikes with a picnic hamper of locally sourced food.

Lapad and Babin Kuk have a network of footpaths that cover most of the peninsula and run along the coast. The Ronald Brown walking trail in Cavtat is a steep uphill climb that rewards hikers with sweeping views of the bay from the summit.

Running

The Dubrovnik international half-marathon takes place in late April/early May and includes a 2km (1.2-mile) dash around the City Walls. Check other running events at www.du-motion.com.

Fishing

Fisherfolk of any level can join a big-game fishing expedition to catch bluefin tuna, amberjack and swordfish. Big Game Fishing (www.dubrovnik-big-game.com) runs half-day and day-long excursions.

Other activities

Adventure companies including Konavle Safari in Cavtat (http://konavlesafari.hr) offer four-hour Jeep safaris driving through the countryside of the Konavle region. This is also the site of a biking and wine tasting excursion offered by Adventure Dalmatia (www.adventure dalmatia.com), which takes in views of the Konavle valley and its villages. Adventure Dalmatia also gives you the thrilling chance to abseil down Dubrovnik's historic City Walls and on to Stradun.

Korčula yachts

Wreck diving

Chronology

From its seventh-century foundation by the Illyrians, through to the Republic of Ragusa, when it was ruled by Venetians, Hungarians and Ottomans, to the twentieth-century conflicts and its present status as part of an independent Croatia and member of the European Union.

Early times

4th century BC Greeks and Illyrians are resident on the coast of Dalmatia.
1st century BC Romans usurp the earlier settlers and establish the colony of Illyricum.
395 After the division of the Roman Empire, Southern Dalmatia comes under the rule of the western half, until its fifth-century collapse.
555 Dalmatia is conquered by Byzantine Emperor Justinian.
9th century Cyril and Methodius, 'the apostles of the southern Slavs', convert the masses to Christianity. Cyril invents the Glagolitic alphabet to translate the Bible into the Slavonic language. St Blaise (Sveti Vlaho) becomes patron saint of the city.

Foreign rule

999 Venetians capture Croatian coast for the first time.
12th century Settlements of Ragusa and Dubrovnik united when Stradun is paved over.
1181 First recorded mention of the Republic of Ragusa.
1202 Fourth Crusade. The Venetians demand the submission of Dubrovnik and install a Venetian as rector.
1358 Under the Peace of Zadar, Hungary gains control of Dubrovnik.
1433 Council of Basel gives papal permission for Dubrovnik to trade with Muslim countries.
1560 Jesuits arrive in Dubrovnik.
15–16th centuries Dubrovnik School of painting flourishes.
1667 Earthquake destroys much of Dubrovnik. Many great works of art are lost.
1806 Napoleon occupies the city. Two years later he dissolves the Republic.

National revival

Mid-19th century Romantic Nationalist Illyrian movement seeks the unification of Southern Slavs.
1905 Stjepan Radić forms the Croatian Peasants' Party.
1919 Under the Versailles Peace Treaty, the Kingdom of Serbs, Croats and Slovenes comes into being, with King Aleksander at its head.
1928 Radić assassinated by a Montenegrin Serb MP.

Example of Glagolitic alphabet

1929 Aleksander forms a dictatorship, calls it the Kingdom of Yugoslavia.
1934 Aleksander assassinated by members of the Ustaše Croatian fascist movement.

World War II to the present day

1941 Axis powers invade Yugoslavia and install the Ustaše in power.
1944 Tito enters Belgrade at head of Red Amy, backed by Allied powers.
1945 Socialist Republic of Yugoslavia comes into being.
1953 Tito elected president. Initiates Non-Aligned Movement and decentralises the economy.
1960s Tourist industry flourishes as visitors descend on the city.
1980 Death of Tito.
1979 Dubrovnik declared a UNESCO World Heritage Site.
1990 Franjo Tuđman elected president, at the head of the Croatian Democratic Union (HDZ).
1991 Break-up of Federal Republic.
1991–92 Homeland War. Dubrovnik besieged.
1990s Rebuilding of damaged city goes ahead; tourist industry flourishes.
1999 Death of Tuđman.
2003 HDZ returns to power under more moderate president Stjepan Mesić and prime minister Ivo Sanader. Croatia applies for EU membership.
2009 Croatia joins Nato.
2012 Sanader convicted of corruption charges.

Kolinda Grabar-Kitarović, 2015–2020 president

2013 Croatia joins the European Union on 1 July.
2015 Kolinda Grabar-Kitarović of the centre-right HDZ party becomes the first female president in the post-independence era.
2017 Dubrovnik's newly elected mayor Mato Franković (HDZ) enforces a cap on the number of tourists visiting the Old Town.
2023 Croatia adopts the euro and is admitted into the Schengen Area.
2024 Dubrovnik reaches record tourist numbers with 1.35 million visitors, a nine percent increase compared to the same period in 2023.

Croatia adopted the euro in 2023

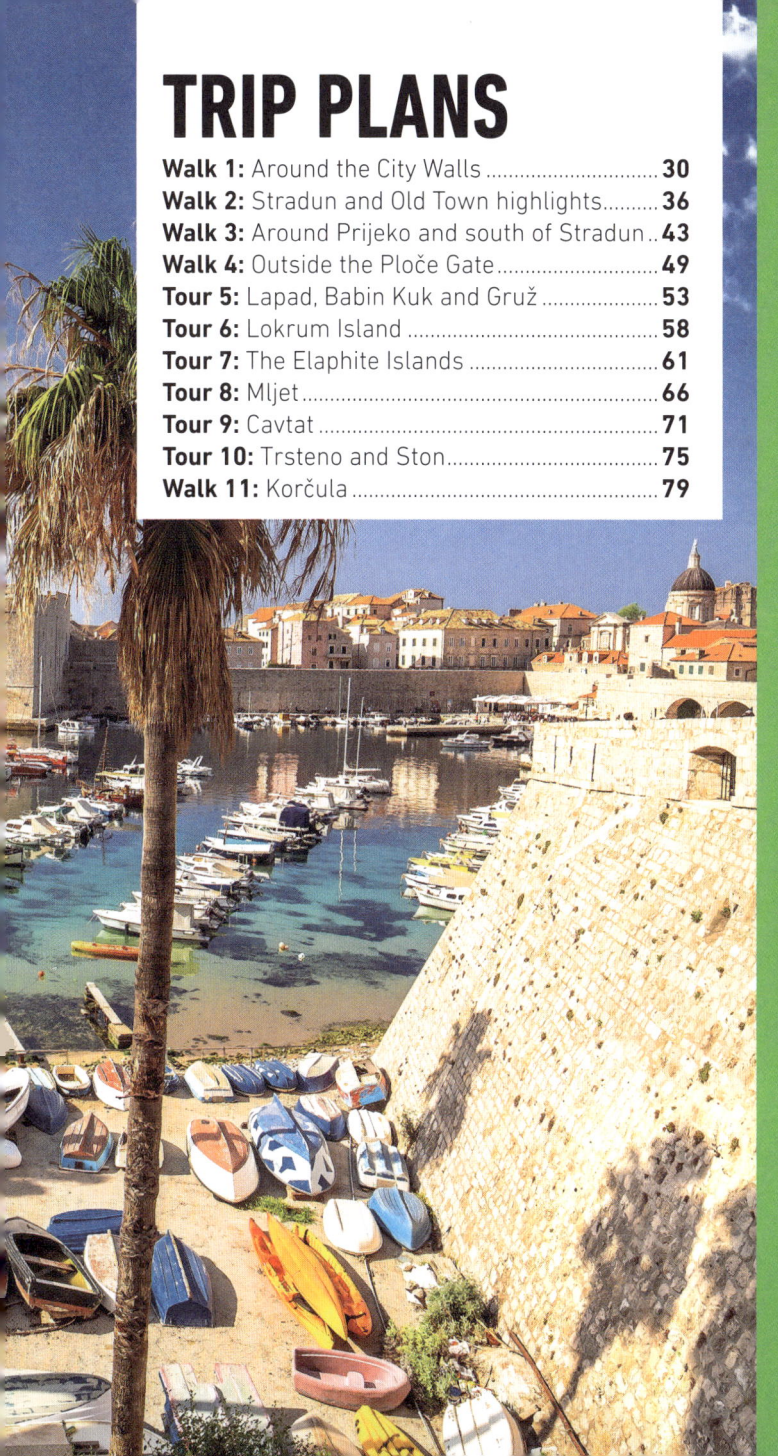

TRIP PLANS

Walk 1: Around the City Walls **30**
Walk 2: Stradun and Old Town highlights.......... **36**
Walk 3: Around Prijeko and south of Stradun.. **43**
Walk 4: Outside the Ploče Gate............................. **49**
Tour 5: Lapad, Babin Kuk and Gruž **53**
Tour 6: Lokrum Island **58**
Tour 7: The Elaphite Islands **61**
Tour 8: Mljet **66**
Tour 9: Cavtat **71**
Tour 10: Trsteno and Ston...................................... **75**
Walk 11: Korčula **79**

WALK 1
Around the City Walls

One of the best ways to start a visit to Dubrovnik is by taking a walk around the City Walls to get a feeling for the layout and the history of the city. This walk also includes Fort Lovrijenac and Dance church, just outside the walls.

DISTANCE: 2km (1.2 miles)
TIME: A full day
START: Outside the Pile Gate
END: Pile Gate
POINTS TO NOTE: If you're staying in Lapud, Babin Kuk or Gruž, you can take bus No. 4, 5 or 6 to reach the Pile Gate. Start as early as you can to avoid the midday heat and the tour group crowds. Remember to bring a hat, water and sunblock; you can get refreshments on the way round although you'll end up paying a premium for them. Entrance is payable in euros and by credit card. Don't leave the walls until you have finished your walk as you will have to pay another entrance fee if you wish to return.

There is usually a bit of a scrum outside the **Pile Gate** ❶ as passengers are disgorged from tour group buses. Above it all, a figure of Sveti Vlaho (St Blaise), the city's patron, holding a model of Dubrovnik, looks down with a benign expression. Through the gate and down a few steps is the inner gate, and immediately to the left, inside the fortifications, is one of the three entrances to the **City Walls** (https://citywallsdubrovnik.hr; ticket also gives admission to Fort Lovrijenac; charge).

Western views

As you climb the long flight of stone steps you can catch sight of the roofs and cloister of the **Franciscan Monastery** ❷ (see walk 2) before turning left. The route is a one-way system that goes anti-clockwise around the walls. **Fort Lovrijenac** looms ahead to your right on the headland across the bay.

To your left you can catch a glimpse of the everyday life of Dubrovnik, with narrow houses, carefully tended, flower-filled gardens, enchanting little roof terraces and children playing ball. The damage from the 1991 siege is hardly visible nowadays as many of the terracotta rooftops have been replaced over the years. Soon you see the circular **Bokar Fortress** ❸, designed

Peeking through the City Walls

in the fifteenth century by Italian architect Michelozzo Michelozzi, jutting out into the sea. As you veer to the left there's the first refreshment stop, a tiny kiosk that sells cold drinks.

South side of the city

Here the island of Lokrum slides into view on your right. Some of the houses beyond the walls are so close that you can peer into their windows, but you might want to resist the temptation. Before you reach the next fortress, **Sveta Margarita** ❹, you can catch views of the chapel to the rear of St Mary's Convent and the Jesuit Church among the neat vegetable gardens.

Near the fortress there's a small souvenir shop and Caffe on the Wall with tables set outside if you want to stop for a drink. Ahead you'll see pinned to the outer wall of the next fortress, **Sveti Stjepan** ❺, a figure of St Blaise, and perhaps wonder how he was manoeuvred and fixed in this seemingly precarious position.

As you approach **Sveti Spasitelj Fortress** ❻ you'll see **Caffe Bar Salvatore** (see ❶), which teems with visitors enjoying the shade of the café umbrellas in the height of the season. Just as popular are the public toilets here, which are the only free public ones in the Old Town.

Maritime Museum

Arriving on the western side of the walls, you see Sveti Ivan Fortress, which

> ## City Walls tips
> This is one of the most popular attractions in Dubrovnik, so be prepared for slow-moving crowds of visitors if you go in high season. To make an attempt at evading the worst of the crowds, be prepared to start the walk the minute the ticket office opens at 8am, as the cruise-ship visitors will descend shortly after that. Or time it for very late afternoon. The paths can be quite narrow and the walls are relatively low; this could be a problem if you have difficulty with heights. Most importantly, wear sturdy flat shoes to cope with the numerous stone staircases throughout the walk.

was built in the fourteenth century and now houses the **Maritime Museum** ❼ (Pomorski Musej; http://dumus.hr/en/maritime-museum; charge). Laid out over two spacious floors, the air-conditioned museum gives an interesting glimpse into the history of this maritime city. There are models of sixteenth-century carracks and galleons, an illuminated view of the port before the Great Earthquake of 1667 (the original painting is in the Franciscan Monastery collection), pictures of nineteenth- and early twentieth-century steamships and their masters, and photographs of boats burning in the harbour during the 1991–92 siege.

Sea view from the walls

The Harbour

Follow the walls now above the harbour, busy with the traffic of small craft coming and going to Cavtat and Lokrum. To your left, you look down on the rear of the ancient churches of St Nicholas and St Sebastian, before reaching the **Ploče Gate** entrance,

City rooftops, old and new

of handmade lace products laid out at the bottom of the steps.

As you round a bend in the walls, your views out to sea are over the Revelin Fortress, the Lazareti and the coast stretching down towards Cavtat. You also get a bird's-eye view of the 360° restaurant terrace at Revelin.

Below are the rooftops of the Dominican Monastery and its Gothic-Renaissance bell tower. Begun in 1390, this tower, with its two great bells, dominates the city, although it faces stiff competition from the Cathedral's lantern dome and the great bulk of the Jesuit Church.

To your left is the upper entrance to the **Dulčić Masle Pulitika Gallery** ❽ (www.ugdubrovnik. hr; charge), which showcases works by Croatian artists Ivo Dulčić, Antun Masle and Đuro Pulitika. It's also the location of the Ronald Brown Memorial House.

Northern views

The next fortress, **Sveti Jakova** ❾, is the third entrance to the City Walls. As you continue along the north side of the city, all the views are breathtaking, and you will have to squeeze your way through the crowds if you're there in high season. This is the classic panorama of Dubrovnik's terracotta rooftops, with Lokrum in the background.

which is one of the three entrances to the walls. After you've finished your walk, you can come back to the gate and check out the colourful displays

City Wall shadows

The view towards the Old Port

Soon you reach the highest point on the walls, the **Minčeta Fortress** ❿, designed and built, like the Rector's Palace, by Michelozzo Michelozzi and Dalmatian Juraj Dalmatinac. By this point in the tour, you will have walked up and down numerous steps, but this final climb to the top of the tower is worth it for the views.

As you descend, you get a closer peek into the cloister of the Franciscan Monastery before you reach street level and the end of the circuit.

Fort Lovrijenac

This walk will probably have taken you 1.5 to 2 hours, so you might want a cool drink before you go any further. Refill your bottle with the clean and refreshing water that gushes out of the **Onofrio fountain** in front of the City Walls ticket office. The next stage of the walk takes you out of the Pile Gate and down Svetoga Đurđa, the narrow alley beside Brsalje square. You reach a tiny chapel (Sv. Đurđa) at one side of Brsale bay, where there's a little fishing jetty. The **Orhan Restaurant** (see ❷) sits on the other side of the bay, at the foot of 165 steps that must be climbed to reach **Fort Lovrijenac** ⓫. Above the entrance to the fortress an inscription reads 'Non Bene Pro Toto Libertas Venditur Auro' (Freedom should not be sold for all the treasure in the world). This massive, early sixteenth-century structure was regarded as vital to the defence of the city, and its commander, like the Republic's rectors, was changed on a monthly basis to prevent an opportunist from gaining a power base and staging a coup. The leaders of the Ragusan Republic, it seems, were cautious to the point of paranoia. The fort featured in the hugely popular *Game of Thrones* series and is the venue for performances of *Hamlet* during the Summer Festival (www.dubrovnik-festival.hr; charge). A more dramatic setting for the tragedy would be hard to imagine.

Dance Church

Back down the many steps now for a well-deserved lunch on the vine-clad terrace of the Orhan Restaurant. If you come at the weekend, it's advisable to book in advance. Afterwards, follow the narrow road called Od Tabakarije through a pretty little neighbourhood and up a hill. Ahead of you, where the roads Frana Bulića and Dante Alighieri meet, stands an imposing building belonging to the Dubrovnik University. Turn left and follow the road through a car park atop a headland, then down a pine-shaded slope where the air is scented with herbs.

You will soon reach the **Franciscan Convent and Church of Dance** ⓬, built on the site of a medieval colony

The impressive fortifications

for people affected by leprosy. There is a well-tended garden here and a little cemetery. The convent is still a functioning one and there are usually nuns around who will let you into the church, but this cannot be guaranteed. The main reason to come here is to see the Lovro Dobričević polyptych (1465) above the altar, one of only three of this artist's works to have survived. Respect the nuns' silent prayer and meditation, and remember to drop a little something in the donations box to the right of the door before you leave. If for any reason you can't gain access to the church, your journey will not have been wasted, because it is a peaceful and beautiful spot, filled with the sound of birdsong.

Journey's End

From here, you could take the path down to the cove below, a popular swimming spot. Or you can go back up to the car park and turn left, to find yourself in a shady and usually empty park – **Gradac** ⓭ – where there is a small fish pond and fountain, benches set beneath the trees, and views out to sea. From the park, follow Frana Bulića back to the university and take the right-hand fork down Dante Alighieri. If you're feeling hungry, turn right on to the busy Braniteija Dubrovnika towards **Pizzeria Tomato** (see ❸). This is very close to the **Wine Museum** (www.winemuseumdubrovnik;

> ## Food and drink
>
> ❶ **Caffe Bar Salvatore**
> Gradska Zidine bb; 098
> 1698 062; €–€€
> Once you've accepted the fact that you'll be surrounded by people and will have paid over the odds for a cold drink, relax and bask in gorgeous views of Lokrum from the top of the City Walls.
>
> ❷ **Orhan Restaurant**
> Od Tabakarije 1;
> www.restaurant-orhan.com; €€–€€€
> Hidden away by the water's edge beneath Fort Lovrijenac, Orhan serves excellent fish and seafood indoors or outside on a small, vine-draped terrace. Best to book in high season.
>
> ❸ **Pizzeria Tomato**
> Brsalje ulica 4; 020-313 092; €
> Along with classic pizzas and salads, you can try the Dubrovnik speciality *soparnik*, a pizza-shaped thin pastry pie filled with chard, olive oil and garlic.

charge) which opened in 2024 in the former summer home of the aristocratic Pucić family just outside the Pile Gate. Its elegant rooms tell the fascinating story of winemaking in the Dubrovnik region.

Pile Gate provides the most dramatic entrance to the Old Town

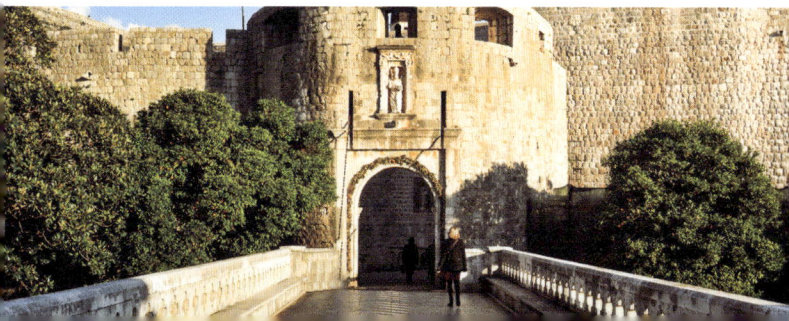

WALK 2
Stradun and Old Town highlights

You haven't seen Dubrovnik until you've explored its historic heart of marble and gleaming Baroque architecture wedged within the old City Walls. And its main artery, Stradun, is simply one of the most beautiful streets in Europe.

DISTANCE: 1km (0.6 miles)
TIME: A full day
START: Outside the Pile Gate
END: Gundulić Square
POINTS TO NOTE: This could be spread out over two days if you want to pace yourself and avoid getting saturated with museums and churches. Most museums close on Monday, but many open every day in summer.

To many, **Stradun** ❶ – also known as Placa – *is* Dubrovnik, that glistening marble-paved thoroughfare that runs between Pile and Ploče Gates. This walk takes a leisurely tour along this main artery and off to the many museums, galleries and squares within the walls of the old town, all of which is pedestrianised.

As you cross Pile Gate's drawbridge and enter through the inner and outer gates, immediately to your right is the domed fifteenth-century Large Onofrio Fountain. It was named after the Italian engineer Onofrio della Cava, who masterminded Dubrovnik's first mains water supply. Behind the fountain is the huge cloister of St Clare's Convent.

The Franciscan Monastery

On the left-hand side of **Stradun**, by the entrance to the City Walls (see walk 1) is the Sveti Spas (Church of Our Saviour), which is often closed in the day but is the venue for chamber music concerts on summer evenings. Next door is the **Franciscan Monastery and Museum** ❷ (Musej Franjevačkog Samostana; charge; see page 30). On your left, inside the main entrance, is a delightful, old – but still functioning – **pharmacy** with ornate shelves and ceramic jars. Then you step into the beautiful Romanesque-Gothic cloister, where capitals on the slender columns are decorated with human and animal figures and floral motifs. These survived the earthquake of 1667, which damaged the monastery and church, and the nineteenth-century depredations when French and

Stradun at dusk

Austrian troops were barracked here at different times and used the cloister to stable their horses. Frescoes depicting the life of St Francis and his arrival in Dubrovnik decorate the walls; in the centre, where herbs for the original pharmacy used to be grown, a statue of the saint stands on a fountain.

Within the **museum** are some fine paintings, among which a fifteenth-century polyptych featuring St Blaise, by Lovro Dobričević, stands out. There is also a collection of reliquaries and chalices and some splendid fifteenth-century illustrated manuscripts. In the pharmacy section, reinstated in its original position, ancient jars, bowls and implements are displayed. The monastery was hit by numerous shells during the 1991–92 siege, and the hole pierced in the wall by one missile shot has been preserved behind glass.

You pass from the monastery into the **church** (free if entered from the street), where the altars are Baroque replacements for those destroyed in the seventeenth-century earthquake. Above the main one is a fine marble *Christ Resurrected* by Ivan Toschini (c.1712), and the altar of Anthony of Padua is surrounded by a delightful painting by Ivo Dulčić (1916–75), installed here in 1962. To the left of the main altar a plaque commemorates the revered poet Ivan Gundulić (1589–1638), who is buried here. Best of all, however, is the *Pietà* outside, above the main (south) door – a lovely, soulful piece that managed to survive the earthquake and subsequent fire.

Stradun and Luža Square

Back in the bustle of Stradun you can stop by the perennially popular **Café Festival** (see ❶). Although Stradun gets crowded when cruise ship groups are being shepherded around, it's a great street to stroll along; you can admire the uniform curved doorways and green shuttered windows of the elegant buildings, and watch reflections dance in the mirror-like surface of the street. There are two good bookshops, a small gallery or two, and a couple of shops selling high-quality clothes as well as plenty of souvenir shops.

The narrow lanes off Stradun are full of inviting bars, tiny restaurants, galleries and shops clinging to the stone steps that eventually lead to Prijeko. If you want a quiet stop for coffee, turn left into Palmotićeva towards **Glam Café** (see ❷). Opposite is D'Vino wine bar (www.dvino.net), one of the city's most convivial places to spend the evening.

Stradun is not a long street, and soon you reach the far end, **Luža Square**, where **Orlando's Column** ❸ stands in the centre, as it has since 1418. Orlando is also known as Roland, as in the medieval epic *Chanson de Roland*. The story linking him with the defence of Ragusa in the ninth century is without any foundation whatsoever, and chronologically impossible, but he has become a much-loved symbol of freedom. Straight ahead of you as you stand at Orlando's feet is the great **Clock Tower**, its bell chimed by the hammers of little green men, and with a rather anachronistic digital clock below. Beneath the clock, to the right, is the **Small Onofrio Fountain**, designed, like the larger one, by della Cava, a pretty little creation, popular with pigeons and as a backdrop for tourists' photographs.

Sponza Palace and St Blaise

To the left is a rare survivor of the 1667 earthquake, the **Sponza Palace** ❹ (https://dad.hr/?lang=en; free), with the single word Dogana on the metal studded door indicating that this used to be the customs house. Now home to the state archive, this is a beautiful building, the delicate windows Venetian Gothic, the main doorway and upper floor late Renaissance, designed by Pasko Miličević and executed by the Andrijić brothers, the renowned Korčula stonemasons. Inside you can admire a narrow, galleried courtyard, and see the original mechanism from the Clock Tower standing rather forlornly at the end, but leave time to visit the **Memorial Room of Dubrovnik Defenders** (free) to the left as you go in. Here, photos of those who died in the 1991–92 siege, many of them heartrendingly young men, are positioned around the walls. Above them are pictures of burning boats and buildings, while a video plays scenes of devastation.

Marble-paved Stradun

Back in the square the **Church of Sveti Vlaho** (St Blaise) is a baroque structure with an interior that is relatively restrained. As the church of the city's patron, it is a favourite place for weddings and baptisms. Within, there's an early eighteenth-century *Martyrdom of St Blaise* on the organ loft and, on the main altar, a silver statue of Blaise holding a model of the city, which shows what it looked like before the earthquake. The fact that this was the only statue in the church to survive the tremor was taken as evidence of the saint's powers. The stained-glass windows, depicting saints Peter and Paul, Cyril and Methodius, are by Ivo Dulčić (1916–75), one of Dubrovnik's most renowned modern artists.

To the left of the church are the imposing buildings of the **Gradska Vijećnica** (Town Hall), the ornate red-and-gold **Marin Držič Theatre** and the **Gradska Kavana** (Town Café; www.nautikarestaurants.com), within the arches of the old arsenal. With a cavernous interior and broad terraces facing on to the square and the port on the other side, the Gradska Kavana is a Dubrovnik institution. Its building also includes the adjoining Arsenal Restaurant and Wine Bar, and the first-floor Kinematografi cinema (http://kinematografi.org), which shows many Hollywood movies in English, as well as Croatian films.

If you're in the mood for lunch at this point, nip into the penultimate narrow lane on the left before Sponza Palace, Kovačka, for a hearty and inexpensive lunch at **Dundo Maroje** (see ❸).

The Old Port

Walk through the gateway between the Sponza Palace and the Clock Tower to the **Old Port** ❺, where you can take in the glorious views of the harbour and the coastline. It's a bustling place, with restaurants, ice-cream stands, craft stalls and the constant coming and going of small boats shuttling to and from Lokrum and Cavtat.

The Rector's Palace

Back in the square, the next on the left is the **Rector's Palace** ❻ (Knežev Dvor; www.dumus.hr), home to the Cultural History Museum. The two earlier versions of the palace – the second of which was designed by Onofrio della Cava, who built the fountains – were both destroyed in fairly quick succession in the fifteenth century by gunpowder explosions in the nearby arsenal, an expensive example of not learning from experience. The current palace, incorporated into the remains by Florentine Michelozzo Michelozzi (1396–1472), has a stunning loggia with intricately carved capitals – both Gothic and Renaissance – atop pillars of Korčula marble. One of the figures on the far-right capital is thought to represent Aesculapius, the god of

Orlando's Column

The bustling harbour

healing. Inside, the atrium, also a harmonious mixture of Gothic and Renaissance, is the venue for Summer Festival events (www.dubrovnik-festival.hr) and for regular concerts by the Dubrovnik Symphony Orchestra (www.dso.hr) throughout the summer. The acoustics are excellent, and it is a magical setting in which to hear music on a summer's night. The bust in the centre commemorates Miho Pracat, the Lopud merchant and mariner who left his entire estate to the Republic and was the only commoner immortalised in this way. Confusingly, the Italian version of Pracat's name – Michaeli Prazotto – is given on the statue.

Visiting the museum, you are directed to the right, through a room containing sixteenth-century portraits, mostly unattributed, then into the Court Room where there are explanations, in English, about how the court functioned during the Republic. Stairs lead down to a vaulted room where there are excellent portraits of Ivan Gundulić and of mathematician Marin Getaldić (1568–1626), friend and contemporary of Galileo, who conducted experiments in a cave not far from the Ploče Gate. Adjoining this room are the former prison cells, with carved wooden chests and statuary, including a fifteenth-century St Blaise from the palace doorway. Back in the atrium, you ascend the wide staircase, where the wooden handrail is supported by huge stone hands, to visit the splendid reconstructed state rooms whose mullioned windows overlook the street and Cathedral. The Republic's rectors, each elected for only one month at a time to prevent them from getting too uppity, were not allowed to leave the palace during their period of office or move their families in with them, but at least they lived in comfort. The Rector's Study (complete with a red-robed model rector) displays a lovely *Baptism of Christ* (1509) by Mihajlo Hamzić.

The Cathedral

Back in the street, you can't miss the imposing, lantern-domed **Cathedral** ❼ (https://katedraladubrovnik.hr). The original Romanesque building, said to have been financed by Richard the Lionheart after he was shipwrecked on Lokrum, was destroyed in the 1667 earthquake. Its Baroque replacement, the work of Italian architects Andrea Buffalini and Paolo Andreotti, completed in 1713, is surprisingly simple, although the side altars are somewhat overblown. Above the severe lines of the modern, marble altar (the earlier one was destroyed in another earthquake in 1979) is a School of Titian polyptych.

The Treasury, to the left of the altar, is tiny, and packed with revered objects. Chief among them are an enamelled gold reliquary of St Blaise's head, and reliquaries in delicate gold

The relics of St Blaise, Dubrovnik's patron saint

and silver filigree of his arms and one leg, which are carried in procession around Dubrovnik on the saint's day, 3 February. Numerous other reliquaries are kept here, as is a copy of Raphael's *Madonna della Seggiola* (the original is in the Pitti Palace in Florence). These treasures were first kept in St Stephen's Church, taken to the Revelin Fortress after the 1667 earthquake, then moved to the Dominican Monastery before being brought here on St Blaise's day in 1721.

Contemporary art

Opposite the Cathedral, built into the city wall, is the **Dulčić Masle Pulitika Gallery** ❽ (www.ugdubrovnik.hr; charge), a small gallery dedicated to three local artists: Ivo Dulčić (1916–75), whose stained-glass windows you can see in St Blaise's as well as his mosaic altarpiece in the Dominican church; Antun Masle (1919–67), some of whose work is also in the Dominican monastery's collection; and Đuro Pulitika, who lived in Dubrovnik until his death in 2006 at the age of 84, and whose delightfully simple Holy Family hangs in the Dominican church. The collection and the changing exhibitions are small but worth seeing if you are interested in contemporary art. You will probably notice the influence of these artists on many of the paintings in small private galleries around the town.

The gallery (also accessible from the top of the walls) is housed on the upper floors of the Ronald Brown Memorial House. Brown, the first African-American US Secretary of Commerce, was the leader of an American trade delegation to Croatia whose plane crashed on the mountainside above Cavtat in 1996. You can peep into a room to the left of the entrance, where photographs of Brown and the 34 people who died with him, along with a roll of honour, are displayed, but the door is rarely open.

Gundulić Square

Go round the back of the Cathedral now, and you will find yourself in Bunićeva Poljana, a square full of café tables – and, at night, usually full of noise and music, as it's a popular meeting place. On one corner is the **Troubadour Jazz Brasserie**, where live jazz is played most evenings. This square leads into another, larger one, **Gundulićeva Poljana** (Gundulić Square) ❾, named after the seventeenth-century writer who symbolised Croatian national identity, not only in his own time, but again during the nineteenth-century nationalist revival and the conflicts of the late twentieth century. His statue stands on a plinth in the centre of the square, a handy perch for the resident pigeons who show him no reverence whatsoever.

Rector's Palace

Food and drink

① Café Festival
Placa bb; www.cafefestival.com; €
There's much scope for people-watching in this prime spot by the Pile Gate. It serves food all day, but it's just as good to soak up the atmosphere over a coffee at one of the outdoor tables.

② Glam Café
Palmotićeva 5; www.facebook.com/glamdu?_rdr; €
This intimate little bar off Stradun is the place for a quiet coffee and a reviving smoothie, where tables squeeze into the narrow stairs going up towards Prijeko. It's a different scene in the evening when people stop by for cocktails.

③ Dundo Maroje
Kovačka bb; www.dundomaroje.com; €–€€
Just off Stradun in a narrow alley by Luža Square is this attractive little restaurant serving pizzas, salads, simply grilled fish and classic seafood pasta and risotto dishes. Meat-eaters aren't left out either with Dalmatian steaks and grilled lamb on the menu.

④ Cele Brunch & Bar
Placa 1; www.celedubrovnik.com; €–€€
You're in the thick of the Stradun action by the Sponza Palace, where tables spill out into Luža Square and live music is played in the evenings. You have the best view for when residents take their evening stroll after the cruise crowds have gone.

Gundulić Square has two separate identities, depending on the time of day you come here. In the morning it is the setting for a lively local market, full of colourful fruit, vegetable and flower stalls, together with a few offering embroidered linen, herbs and lavender. By 1pm, there is scarcely a sign left of this activity, and tables, chairs and sun umbrellas are set out by waiters from a line of restaurants. If you didn't have lunch earlier, this would be a great place for it, or you could return here for an evening meal, when the area is equally lively.

You've reached the end of the itinerary, but if you feel it's time for coffee and cake, go back to **Cele Brunch & Bar** on the corner of Stradun, which does cream cakes (see ④). If you sit for a while longer, or return here in the evening, you will have a grandstand view of the Croatian version of the Italian *passeggiata* known as the *džir* – strolling up and down the street, stopping to talk to friends, or having a drink or ice cream at a café table while their invariably well-dressed children play ball, ride bikes or chase each other over the shiny paving stones.

Ivan Gundulić monument

WALK 3
Around Prijeko and south of Stradun

This leisurely walk combines an exploration of the hilly streets north of Stradun with a stroll through the lanes near the southern side of the City Walls. There's also a chance to swim on a rocky beach.

DISTANCE: 1.5km (0.9 miles)
TIME: Three hours
START: Luža Square
END: Gundulić Square
POINTS TO NOTE: There are opportunities to extend the walk by stopping for a swim, or for a drink with a spectacular sea view. Take a swimming kit if you want to drop into the sea to cool off, and flat shoes are best for the numerous flights of steps that make up the streets north of Stradun.

The streets to the north and south of Stradun are full of character, colour and history. North of Stradun are Prijeko and a series of narrow alleyways with several flights of steps that eventually take you under the shadow of the City Walls. South of Stradun is a warren of little lanes decked with flowers and filled with hole-in-the-wall bars and restaurants. It's a place to get lost and stumble upon unexpected paths and corners.

From Luža Square, go through the archway by the Sponza Palace, past stalls offering embroidered cloths and trinkets, and follow Ulica Svetog Dominika for a few metres. To the right, another arch leads out to the Old Port. Straight ahead is a graceful Gothic staircase leading to the monastery. At the top of the steps, on the right, is the **Sebastian Gallery** ❶ (free), where changing exhibitions of modern art are held (and works sold) in the fifteenth-century votive church of St Sebastian. Here the cool, white vaulted rooms make an attractive exhibition space. The gallery also sells beautifully hand-crafted jewellery, much of it made from coral.

The Dominican Monastery

Enter the **Dominican Church and Monastery** ❷ (Dominikanska Crkva i Samostan) through a peaceful cloister, where late-Gothic arcades are embellished with Renaissance motifs. In the centre is a huge well that was last used to supply water

In the shadow of the City Walls

for the besieged city in 1991–92. Like its Franciscan counterpart, the cloister was used in the nineteenth century as barracks and stables both by French and Austrian troops.

Among the excellent paintings in the museum are three by Nikola Božidarević (c.1460–1518): the *Holy Conversation* (1513), showing the *Virgin and Child* with saints and angels; *The Annunciation*, painted some 10 years later; and *The Virgin with Saints*, in which Mother and Child are flanked by saints Blaise and Paul on one side and Dominic and Augustine on the other. Also look out for Mihajlo Hamzić's triptych, commissioned by the wealthy Lukarević family in 1512, showing an avuncular St Nicholas framed by a Renaissance-style shell. There are also a number of illustrated manuscripts and a collection of reliquaries, including one of the

The Dominican Monastery

head of St Stephen, first king of Hungary (997–1038). The church, remodelled in baroque style after the 1667 earthquake, has an attractive stone pulpit, and some modern works of art. These include Ivo Dulčić's mosaic altarpiece, Djuro Pulitika's *Holy Family*, a bronze *Virgin and Child* by Ivan Meštrović, and eye-catching stained-glass windows that replaced those that were shattered during the 1991–92 bombardment.

Prijeko

The street directly opposite the door of St Sebastian is Prijeko, which runs along to the far end of Stradun and is lined with restaurants – many of average quality. On the right is the Church of the Holy Rosary, on the left the tiny chapel of St Nicholas – both usually closed. Pop down the third street on the left – Žudioska – to visit the **Synagogue and Museum** ❸ (Sinagoga Muzej) The museum contains parchment Torah scrolls, said to have been brought here by Sephardic Jews after their expulsion from Spain in 1492, as well as embroidered Torah Ark covers, and a list of Dubrovnik's Jewish victims of the Holocaust. On the second floor is a synagogue – small, but more than large enough to accommodate the dozen or so Jewish families that remain in the city.

Back along Prijeko you will be accosted by waiters inviting you to sit and eat at one of the tables beneath umbrellas – regardless of the time of day.

Images of war

Further along, look out for Antuninska on the left and you will come to the cosy **Caffe Bar Tinel** (see ❶). A few doors further down is **War Photo Limited** ❹ (www.warphotoltd.com), an innovative gallery that displays exhibitions of work by award-winning photographers. Exhibitions change regularly, but there are permanent displays of images from the conflicts in the former Yugoslavia. Gallery owner Frederic Hancez, a Belgian businessman, and New Zealand director Wade Goddard, who first came to the region as a war photographer, aim not to shock or sensationalise, but to show the true face of war and remind us that situations remain unresolved when the world's press moves on. The setting, with its high vaulted ceilings, is as dramatic as the images on display.

There are a couple more little streets this side of Stradun to wander up and down before you emerge once more into the town's main artery. Look out for details in the narrow lanes of steep steps: tiny galleries and little shops, hole-in-the-wall cafés where people sit on cushions outside when there's not enough space for even the smallest table and chairs.

Franciscan monastery

War Photo Limited

South of Stradun

Walk down Stradun towards Ploče and turn right towards the main door of the Cathedral. This district is called Pustjerna, and it's the oldest one in the city. If you're in the mood to amble along, you could nip into some of its arcaded lanes and explore the stony footpaths. But if you're in need of sustenance, stop for a cold drink and some people-watching at **Caffe Bar NoneNina** just before the Cathedral (see ❷).

Turn into Ulica Kneza Damjana Jude in front of the Cathedral, where restaurant tables fill the narrow street. Take a right into Bandureva and another right into Braće Andrijića, past the fifteenth-century Ranjina Palace, a Gothic private residence. The street was named after the Andrijić brothers, who were stonemasons from Korčula, and two streets along, in Restičeva, you will see one of their greatest works, the Renaissance Skočibuha Palace. At the top of Braće Andrijića you come to the foot of the City Walls, where you turn right into Ispod Mira. A short way along, a gateway in the wall leads down a wide rocky path to a concreted bathing area. If you feel like having a swim, this is your chance. Otherwise, continue your walk beneath the walls.

The Jesuit Church

Briefly leave the shadow of the walls when you see, to your right, the great bulk of the **Jesuit Church** ❺ (Crvka Sveti Ignacija; free). Poljana Boškovića, in which it stands, is a slightly untended neighbourhood square with washing hanging outside a few houses and – unlike the church – no pretensions at all. Unless you arrive here when one of the tour groups is visiting, you feel that you could be in a rustic village square, even though you are only about 200 metres/yds from the centre of town. The church was designed by the Jesuit Andrea Pozzo and modelled (inside) on the Gesù Church in Rome. Building work began in 1664, although it was interrupted by the earthquake three years later, and was finally completed in 1725.

You enter through a door flanked by Corinthian columns, to be faced with a massive interior, dominated by marble side altars. The ceiling of the apse, painted by Spanish-Sicilian Gaetano García, shows Ignatius, founder of the Jesuit Order, ascending to heaven amid fluffy white clouds, while the walls are decorated with scenes from his life, and Pozzo's signature trompe l'oeil surrounding them. To the right of the main door is an extremely kitsch Grotto of Lourdes, with a pink-and-white Virgin surrounded by plastic flowers and gazing down on a hopeful pilgrim. At the side of the church is the Jesuit College (Collegium Ragusinum) completed in the 1690s after much controversy. Poet Ivan Gundulić (1589–1638) and mathematician Ruđer Bošković

The impressive bulk of the Jesuit Church

(1711–87), among other prominent Ragusans, were educated here. To the right of the church the Jesuit Steps sweep down towards Gundulić Square.

If you're in the mood to stop for lunch – or plan to return in the evening for an alfresco supper – **Restaurant Kopun** is a good choice (see ❸).

Back to the Walls

Back under the walls, a sign proclaims 'Cold drinks with the most beautiful view' and a short way along, this is exactly what you get. Pop through a hole in the wall to find **Buža Bar** (see ❹) with tables set on terraces cut into the cliff, stunning sea views and the sight of Lokrum ahead. (Bear in mind that the café will be closed if the weather is bad. Once you see the café, you'll understand why the owners wouldn't risk staying open in high winds and rain.) Carry on along Ulica od Kaštela, and allow yourself to be tempted down any of the little stepped streets to your right, bright with flowery window boxes and flapping washing and with impressive stone balconies and decorated stonework on otherwise humble dwellings. The building you soon pass on the left is the former convent of St Mary, now converted into private apartments.

Museums in the back streets

After about 100 metres/yds you can follow the walls no longer and must turn down Na Andriji, which takes a sharp turn to the right and deposits you outside the **Rupe Ethnographic Museum** ❻ (Etnografski Musej Rupe; http://dumus.hr/en). This sixteenth-century building was the store house for the government grain reserves, which were kept in the huge dry wells you can still see in the floors ('rupe' means hole or cavern). Upstairs, the museum displays agricultural implements, fishing paraphernalia and ornate festival costumes. The building and the views from the upper windows are of most interest.

A few metres right of the museum (note the wooden ramps over the steps to enable delivery carts to get up here) take the first left, Od Domina, down past the Domino church. This is usually closed during the day but is the venue for concerts on Sunday evening. Next door is the **Home of Marin Držić** ❼ (Dom Marina Držića; http://muzej-marindrzic.eu; charge). Držić (1508–67) is one of Dubrovnik's most revered playwrights, and his works take pride of place in the Summer Festival. In a missed opportunity, however, the museum does not give a great deal of insight into his life. The collection consists of little more than a video about his time in Siena, theatre posters from his plays, a museum gift shop and a rather quirky (free) audio guide in

Buža Bar's spectacular setting

Food and drink

① Caffe Bar Tinel
Antuninska 5; 099-201 1666; €
Stop for a coffee under the vaulted ceiling of this tiny bar, where the walls are covered with arty photos of its customers as well as some original paintings. When the weather is warm, people while away the evening on comfy cushions that line the steps outside.

② Caffe Bar NoneNina
Pred Dvorom 4; 098-915 9909; €€
At one point or another, most visitors have dropped by NoneNina's – only it was called Hemingway in those days and still is by some people. It's still one of the best people-watching cafés in the city.

③ Restaurant Kopun
Poljana Ruđera Boškovića 7; www.restaurantkopun.com; €€–€€€
Fresh seafood and Dalmatian meat dishes are served in this romantic restaurant opposite the Jesuit Church. It's especially atmospheric on warm evenings when the outdoor tables spill into the square.

④ Buža Bar
Od Margarite; www.bbuza.com; €
You might spend a bit more at Buža than you would normally on a drink, but you're sitting at a bar that's been carved into the cliffs, and the view is sublime. As you would expect, it's busy at sunset in summer when it becomes one of the most coveted places for a sundowner. There's also a smaller Buža Bar slightly further east.

---

a building that gives only a glimpse into life in the sixteenth century.

From the museum, go left along Za Rokum and turn right by a small church to reach Od Puča. Historically the street of the silversmiths, busy little Od Puča still has many shops selling gold and silver filigree jewellery, along with souvenir shops, a couple of little galleries, an old-fashioned barber's and a speciality tea and coffee house. On the left is the plain and partially restored Serbian Orthodox Church (variable hours) and, next door but one, the **Icon Museum** ⑧ (Musej Pravoslavne Crkve; currently closed for renovations). Once the museum reopens, you can explore its interesting collection of Orthodox icons dating from the fifteenth to nineteenth centuries, as well as portraits of local Serbs painted by Vlaho Bukovac. If you continue along the street a little further you will find yourself in Gundulić Square, or take any turning on the left and you will be back in Stradun.

Gundulić Square

WALK 4
Outside the Ploče Gate

This walk from Ploče Gate leads northeast along a quiet coast road, visiting the Museum of Modern Art and ending at a secluded cove, with an optional trip to Mount Srđ.

> **DISTANCE:** 5km (3 miles)
> **TIME:** Half a day
> **START:** Ploče Gate
> **END:** Ploče Gate
> **POINTS TO NOTE:** The walk, with a visit to the museum, can easily be done in two hours, but if you stop for a swim and a drink at one of the beach bars, it could make a satisfying half-day out. If you choose to take the cable car to Mount Srđ it will, of course, take more time. There is a longer, more arduous option to hike up Mount Srđ, which is about a 4km (2.5 miles) walk up a zigzagging path and will take just under an hour each way.

In the height of summer, it can be oppressively busy within the City Walls when the cruise ships dock and passengers descend on the Old Town. Escaping the crowds with a stroll along the shore road gives you a different perspective on the city. And a trip up to Mount Srđ rewards you with sweeping views of the coast.

Ploče Gate and Banje Beach

Outside the **Ploče Gate** ❶, there is a drawbridge and outer and inner gates flanked during the summer months by stoical costumed guards and presided over by St Blaise. On the harbour side is the Culture Club Revelin (www.club revelin.com), whose terrace tables offer splendid views and are great for a morning coffee or a sunset drink. On the other side looms the bulk of the **Revelin Fortress** ❷, built in the sixteenth century to protect the town against Turkish attacks from the interior. Its ground floor houses the Archaeological Museum (www.dumus.hr), which contains medieval sculptures and church furniture as well as displays showing how the fortress was built. Opposite is **Snogu Wok Bar** (see ❶), a handy spot for a plate of spicy Asian street food, including vegan options.

Out on the main road, Frana Supila, the palatial building on your left is a school, as the sounds emanating from inside will tell you. To the right are the walls of the **Lazareti** ❸ (Frana Supila 8; www.lazaretihub.com), which used to be an old quarantine hospital built

Harbour view from Ploče Gate

in the seventeenth century to keep disease from the city. Its half-dozen buildings now form Dubrovnik's premier arts venue spread over three floors and sprawling towards the beach, with a large courtyard tucked within. Local folklore group Linđo often puts on performances here, and the venue features cinema nights when Croatian and international films are projected on the outside walls. It's also home to a late-night club with appearances by live bands and top DJs from around the world. There are a couple of small galleries at street level, and the cavernous rooms below house textile workshops.

Beside a small post office there are steps leading down to pebbly **Banje Beach** ❹, from which you can water-ski. There is another flight of steps further up, near the Hotel Excelsior. Security guards are on duty at either end, but this is a public beach, so you're free to pitch a towel wherever you find a space – or preferably a padded beach mat to protect you from the pebbles. The swish **Banje Beach Club** (www.banjebeach.com) has a cordoned-off section where you can rent canopied loungers if you want a bit of comfort. Because it's the main beach by the Old Town, it gets unbelievably busy in the summer, but the water stays warm until well into the autumn and is a tranquil place out of season.

Museum of Modern Art

Past the beach, on the left-hand side at No. 23, is the **Museum of Modern Art** ❺ (Umjetnička Galerija; http://ug dubrovnik.hr/en; charge). It is housed in a beautiful building that looks pure Renaissance but was actually built in 1935 for a wealthy shipowner. When the doors are closed, it is easy to miss

Banje Beach, Dubrovnik's recreational shore

the gallery, as its name is displayed only on a discreet plaque to the left of the entrance. The collection, housed over four floors, with sculptures in the courtyard, is rotated, but invariably includes works by Vlaho Bukovac (1855–1922), who, in 1878, was the first Croatian to be accepted by the Paris Salon. Bukovac was born in Cavtat where more of his work can be seen. Upstairs the collection moves further into the twentieth century, and includes works by some of the country's best-known modern sculptors, Ivan Kožarić, Frano Kršnić and Ivan Meštrović. There are also paintings by Ivo Dulčić and Đuro Pulitika, although many of these are now shown in the gallery opposite the Cathedral. On the third floor the palatial salon and terrace threaten to outshine the exhibits, and the top floor is used for changing exhibitions.

Folly and philosophy

Almost opposite the gallery is the swanky Hotel Excelsior (www.adriaticluxuryhotels.com), then the interlinked Villa Orsula and Grand Villa Argentina (the latter two are currently closed for renovation, due to reopen in late 2025), where the road divides. Take the lower path, Ulica Vlaha Bukovca, where, in lush gardens, stands an opulent folly known as the **Villa Scheherazade** ❻, built in the early twentieth century for a wealthy banking family. All you see from the road, peering through Mozarabic wrought-iron gates, is the shiny tiled blue dome. But you get an excellent view of the folly from the sea on a boat trip to Lokrum, where it looks like something out of a James Bond film. It used to be a privately owned villa, but it was bought by the Adriatic Luxury Hotels group and offers accommodation at a suitably luxurious price.

Next door, but within the gardens, is a tiny chapel with a bell wall and a plaque on the wall informing passers-by that the mathematician and natural philosopher Marin Getaldić (1568–1626) used to conduct experiments in a cave below (you can see the cave from the sea or when looking back at the end of this walk). Local people were extremely wary of Getaldić, convinced that his activities in the cave must have had something to do with witchcraft.

Walking along this narrow road, with cypresses and century plants growing on the seaward side and oleanders in gardens on the left, you feel as if you are in a country lane. There's little traffic, particularly after you pass the Villa Dubrovnik Hotel, see page 88 (www.villa-dubrovnik.hr). A short way along you reach the square-towered former monastery of Sveti Jakov (St Jacob), now a private residence, except for the church, which is open only for mass on Sunday. Follow the path as it winds down behind the monastery. There are great views back to town (and to Getaldić's cave) and an unmarked flight of steps down to the lovely

The striking Villa Dubrovnik Hotel

Food and drink

🟢 Snogu Wok Bar
Frana Supila 1;
www.facebook.com/snoguwok; €
If you need a quick dose of spicy Asian street food, pick up a box of noodles or rice with all the usual toppings just outside the Ploče Gate. You'll also find vegetarian and vegan options.

---

sheltered beach of Sveti Jakov, which is mainly pebbly with some sandy sections. During the summer there's a snack bar and restaurant, and you can rent kayaks, pedalos and jet skis.

Nostalgic corner

Ahead of you is an old wrought-iron gate on which can just be discerned the words **'Hotel Belvedere'** ❼. Through here, to the left, are the derelict remains of the hotel that suffered so badly in the bombardment of 1991–92. Because it was close to the ridge from which shells and artillery were fired, it stood little chance. A Russian billionaire bought the ruin to convert it into a luxurious hotel, and it was also used as a *Game of Thrones* location. At present, however, it's an eerie, atmospheric spot, especially out of season.

Mount Srđ and the Cable Car

Retrace your steps so that you're near the Ploče Gate. On your right you'll see the sign for the **Dubrovnik Cable Car** ❽ (www.dubrovnikcablecar.com; charge). Walk along Ulica Iza Grada, turn right on to Zagrebačka and right again on to Kralja Petra Krešimira IV. If you are taking the Atlas airport transfer bus (www.atlas-croatia.com) back to the airport, this is where you board for the return journey, not at the Pile Gate.

The 778-metre (2,552ft) journey up to Mount Srđ takes only a few minutes, but views along the way are wonderful as the car climbs up to the ridge. At the cable car station at the top, there's a souvenir shop and the Panorama restaurant. Outside there's an amphitheatre, which, when it's not being used for weddings, gives visitors ample room to roam around and take in the views of the Elaphite Islands, Lokrum and a wide swathe of the Dalmatian coastline down below. Behind is a stark ridge of bare brown mountains, which contrast dramatically with the blue of the Adriatic Sea.

Your ticket to the cable car includes a visit to the **Museum of the Homeland War** ❾ (www.mdrd.hr; charge if you don't have cable car ticket), which is housed in one wing of the remains of Fort Imperial, a Napoleonic fort. The well-documented exhibition is a moving testimony to the suffering and destruction inflicted on the city. There is also a memorial to those who died defending Mount Srđ during the 1991–92 siege of Dubrovnik.

Stupendous views from the cable car

TOUR 5
Lapad, Babin Kuk and Gruž

A tour of the peninsula takes you to the heart of Dubrovnik's summertime playground and some of its most popular beaches. Out of season, the sea views are just as spectacular.

> **DISTANCE:** 12km (7.5 miles)
> **TIME:** Half a day, but longer if you want to spend the day at the beach
> **START:** Pile Gate
> **END:** Pile Gate
> **POINTS TO NOTE:** Although many visitors will be based at the hotels on the peninsulas, for simplicity's sake this tour starts with a 10-minute journey on the No. 6 bus from the Pile Gate.

Most of Dubrovnik's hotels are to be found on the Lapad and Babin Kuk peninsulas, just a short bus ride from the Old Town, and close to Gruž harbour. Although many new developments are changing the face of these suburbs, they remain pleasant, family-friendly, tree-filled areas with delightful bays. This tour will introduce the area and encompass a walk past Lapad Bay and around the Babin Kuk headland.

Lapad's pedestrianised promenade

The bus route runs west from the Pile Gate past the urban bus station and along the southwest side of Gruž harbour, passing the Hotel Lapad see page 90 (www.hotel-lapad.hr) and some magnificent mansions sitting in palm-shaded gardens, to the Orsan Yacht Club. Here it turns away from the harbour and goes uphill, along **Šetalište Kralja Zvonimira**. Get off at the **post office** ❶ (ask for the *pošta*) at the roundabout, cross the main road and walk down the attractive, pedestrianised section of Zvonimira towards the sea. You will pass a number of small hotels and a whole line of cafés with comfortable swing seats set out on the tiled pavement. Near the end of the street, a little promenade leads off to the left, parallel to the beach (it later becomes Masarykov put, a road lined with big hotels that wends its way up to the headland). On the corner is a park with a children's playground and a row of little kiosks selling tickets for boat trips to the islands.

Babin Kuk peninsula

Where Zvonimira meets **Uvala Lapad** ❷ (Lapad Bay, shown as Uvala Sumratin on some maps) you will see

Babin Kuk peninsula

54

TOUR 5 LAPAD, BABIN KUK AND GRUŽ

Most people staying in Dubrovnik will be in one of the large hotels around Lapad

55

TOUR 5 BABIN KUK PENINSULA

500 m / 550 yds

N

Sv. Ignacija
NUNCIJATA

Long Distance Bus Station

Strinčjera 412

Petka
Berkeley
GRUŽ

Uvala Batala

Robna kuća Minčeta
Autobusni kolodvor (Libertas Bus Station)
ŠIPČINE
Jug Stadium

MONTOVJERNA
BONINOVO
GORNJI KONO

Muzej Domovinskog rath (Museum of the Homeland War)

OSPINO POLJE
Lero
Bellevue
Vladimira Nazora
SREDNJI KONO

ostan Svete biteljí muzej
Rixos Libertas Dubrovnik

Rt Gospa

Sv. Danač
PARK BALTAZARA BOGIŠIĆA
Hilton Imperial Dubrovnik
PARK
Inter-University Centre
GRADAC
Tvrđava Lovrijenac (Fort Lovrijenac)
Rt Dance
Vrata od Pila
Tvrđava Bokar
PILE
Tvrđava Minčeta
Franjevački samostan-muzej
STARI GRAD (WORLD HERITAGE)

the big, sleek Hotel Kompas see page 90 (www.adriaticluxuryhotels.com), the Fish & Seafood Restaurant (www.restaurant-casa.com) and the broad beach with its giant concrete slide at the water's edge. You'll also see the beginning of a narrow path on the right that leads westwards along the coast. This is the start of a pleasant walk around the Babin Kuk peninsula, with pine trees framing crystal-clear waters, oleanders drooping from gardens, people fishing from the rocks, cats dozing in the sun and plenty of opportunities to swim from the rocks. Although ladders have been conveniently placed to help you in and out, many of the rocky paths leading to the sea need a certain amount of surefootedness, particularly on the way down.

On your right you'll see the entrance to Restaurant More (www.restaurant-more.com), which belongs to Hotel More, see page 90 (pronounced Mor-eh; www.hotel-more.hr). If you're doing the walk in the late afternoon, this is the place to stop for a drink at the **Cave Bar** (see ❶), which has one of the most stunning interiors you'll see among the local hotels. There's a terrace, too, for alfresco drinks.

At the Levanat restaurant, see page 100 (www.restaurant-levanat.com), the path turns a corner and runs beside the lovely Villa Elita. It carries along the coast to the Hotel Neptun, see page 91 (www.hotelneptundubrovnik.com), where the terrace makes an ideal spot for a drink, especially at sunset. Go round behind the hotel, turn right and then left at the orange Libertas bus sign. You have to make this small detour to avoid the Dubrovnik President/Valamar hotel complex, see page 91 (www.valamar.com), which has colonised the tip of the peninsula.

Babin Kuk's beaches

Now go through a small, family-oriented park, with children's play equipment, table tennis, and benches and stone tables. At the other side, bypass a small shopping centre and follow the path marked 'Plaža/Beach' a short way down to a beach known as **Copacabana** ❸. Here you'll find a sports club, a water chute, pedalos and jet skis for hire, ice-cream sellers and a picturesque café run from a disused chapel. There are very good facilities including showers and changing cabins.

You could stop for a swim or a drink here before carrying on the path before reaching a fork. Veer off to the left and join the narrow pretty path through holm oaks and olive trees, with a view of Daksa island off to the left and the Tuđman Bridge ahead, spanning the estuary. Past a scruffy fishing harbour and the edge of Camping Solitudo (from where you can make diving trips; www.camping-adriatic.com) you come to a line of fishing jetties before the path follows the curve of the coast to the right. It soon joins a residential street and, after a few minutes, you'll see

Copacabana beach

Food and drink

❶ Cave Bar
Nika I Meda Pucića 13;
www.cavebar-more.com; €
The cave in question at the Hotel More's bar was discovered when the hotel was being built, and it lends a highly atmospheric touch to this popular meeting point for guests and non-guests alike. The view from the outdoor terrace overlooking the sea is just as captivating as the grotto-like interior, making it a prime spot for a sundowner.

❷ TIME Bar & More
Iva Vojnovića 39; 099-589 9909; €
Dubrovnik's younger set has colonised this lively music bar. If you're staying in Lapad and want a change from the hotel bars, it's worth a visit to TIME or its equally lively neighbour Caffe Bar What's Up (www.instagram.com/caffewhatsup).

❸ Amfora
Obala Stjepana Radića 26;
https://amfora-restaurant.com; €€
It's only a short stroll from Gruž harbour to Amfora, where they show an assured touch with grilled meats, seafood dishes and pastas. Try to get a table on the upstairs terrace, if it's open.

---

the **Orsan Yacht Club** ❹ on the left. From here you can either take a sharp right up Zvonimira and back to Lapad Bay, or continue along the side of the harbour, back towards the bus station.

Alternatively, check out the row of bars and cafés on Ulica Iva Vojnovića that have become the places to flock to in Lapad away from the tourist hot spots. **TIME Bar & More** (see ❷) is one of the most popular. They're all on the Nos 2, 5, 7 and 9 bus routes.

Gruž

Gruž, across the water, has been quietly developing a reputation as Dubrovnik's hippest district. Here, the **Red History Museum** ❺ (Muzej Crvene Povijesti; www.redhistorymuseum.com; charge) tells the story of communist Yugoslavia in engaging hands-on exhibits that perfectly balance kitsch with deadly seriousness. Its courtyard hosts pop-up events, exhibitions and vintage markets.

As well as Gruž's fruit, vegetable and fish markets (Mon–Sat morning), it is the place to catch the Jadrolinija ferries to Mljet and Korčula and onwards to Split. It's also where the giant cruise ships dock. The long-distance bus station (Autobusni Kolodvor) is a short way from the harbour. Like Lapad, Gruž is opening more restaurants and cafés, including more that offer vegetarian and vegan menus. **Amfora** (see ❸) is worth seeking out.

Looking across towards Gruž and its giant cruise ships

TOUR 6
Lokrum Island

This tiny island of forested footpaths and beaches is only a 15-minute boat journey from Dubrovnik's harbour, but it feels a world away from the bustle of the Old Town.

DISTANCE: 3km (1.8 miles)
TIME: Half a day
START: Dubrovnik Old Port
END: Dubrovnik Old Port
POINTS TO NOTE: Boats make the 15-minute journey every hour from the Old Port in summer. Some boats to Cavtat also stop off at Lokrum. It can make a leisurely half-day or even a day trip, if you take a picnic or opt to eat in the restaurant. Take swimming things, sunblock and sensible shoes, and don't forget to check the time of the last boat back. If you want to picnic, pick up some freshly baked savoury pastries at the Babić bakery on Frana Supila just outside the Ploče Gate.

Lokrum is a peaceful, undeveloped little island. It is scarcely 2km (1.2 miles) long, and most things of interest to visitors are within 500 metres/yds of the harbour. However, its chief attraction is its tranquillity and calming greenery. When you arrive at the jetty, there's a map of the island (but none on sale) and a desk where a small entry charge is made, although this is waived for passengers from the regular ferry service.

Legends of Lokrum

Legend has it that Richard the Lionheart was shipwrecked here on his way back from the crusades at the end of the twelfth century and, in gratitude for his survival, built a votive chapel on the island and financed the construction of Dubrovnik's Cathedral. There is no real evidence for this story, but there may be a grain of truth in it somewhere.

Another legend tells of a curse placed on Lokrum by Benedictine monks in 1808, after the French governor, put in charge by Napoleon when he dissolved the Ragusan Republic, closed the monastery that had been established there in the eleventh century. French rule over Dubrovnik did not last long, and when authority passed to the Austro-Hungarian Empire, it seems the curse went with it. Maximilian, brother of Emperor Franz Josef,

The wooded island is the easiest excursion from Dubrovnik

bought the island in 1859, converted the monastery and established a botanical garden, which is still there today. Some five years later, however, Maximilian was sent off to Mexico as emperor, a position he held only until 1867, when he was executed.

Next in line for the curse was Crown Prince Rudolf, son of Franz Josef, who took over the island a dozen years later, but died by suicide in 1889. The lure of Lokrum remained strong, however, and in 1914 Archduke Franz Ferdinand and his wife Sophie planned to spend the summer there. Unfortunately, they went first to Sarajevo, where they were assassinated, and the world was plunged into war.

Monastery

Today, Lokrum seems more blessed than cursed. From the jetty at **Portoč** ❶, walk the short distance to the remains of the **monastery** ❷, where there's a family-run restaurant in the cloister, and fig trees cling to the crumbling walls. Be careful if you have children with you: a huge cistern just outside the cloister is inadequately fenced off. A few hundred metres southeast of the monastery is the **Mrtvo More** ❸ (Dead Sea), a shallow saltwater lagoon surrounded by flowery shrubs and filled with clear warm water – ideal for swimming. You can also swim off the rocks here and at several other points around the island. Those who prefer calm waters will opt for the lagoon, the little beach near the harbour or the rocky beach on the west coast near the public toilets. Those in search of solitude or more challenging waves will head for the rocks on the southern side. If you find the rocky terrain tough to cope with, you can buy a sponge mat from the kiosk to make lying in the sun more enjoyable. There is also a naturist beach at the southern tip of the island, so look out for the 'FKK' sign if you wish to find it or avoid it.

Botanical Gardens

Back towards the monastery is the signposted path to the **Botanical Gardens** ❹, somewhat overgrown but lush and lovely, as is most of the island. Descendants of the peacocks introduced by Maximilian strut the paths and squawk from their perches in the trees, totally unconcerned by the presence of humans.

Game of Thrones fame

Fans of the television series *Game of Thrones* will be very familiar with Lokrum, as the island is the setting for the fictional city of Qarth. There is now a tiny museum displaying some of the paraphernalia from the series, including the iron throne itself, in the Benedictine monastery.

Fort Royal

If you have the energy you can also climb up to the ruined **Fort Royal** ❺, built by the French on a hill to the west of the monastery (also signposted). There's not a great deal left of the structure, but the views are splendid and you will be accompanied on your way by butterflies flitting around you and bird calls from above. Be aware of the gaps in the ruins: they're not fenced in and there's no warning of any gaping holes.

Forest of holm oak

While you could whizz round the island in a couple of hours, it's worth taking your time strolling through the forested paths taking in the scent of Aleppo pines. Just to the east of Fort Royal is a path through a **forest of holm oak** ❻, which leads back to the jetty. Olive trees are scattered around the island, offering blissful shade on a hot day. Part of Lokrum's charm is the fact that no one is allowed to sleep on the island: there's no hotel or campsite, just peace and quiet.

Food and drink

There are two restaurants next to the monastery. Rajski Vrt is in a lovely spot in the shade and serves a touristy fare of burgers, pasta and pizzas. Lacroma is a much more elegant affair, serving fine Mediterranean cuisine. There is also a small snack bar near the harbour and the Lake Cocktail Bar near the saltwater lagoon. Many visitors bring a picnic, though, as there's no shortage of places in the shade or on the rocky beach to eat.

Peacocks roam freely in the Botanical Gardens

TOUR 7
The Elaphite Islands

Spend a day island-hopping from Koločep to Šipan and Lopud – three peaceful and pretty Elaphite Islands that lie just north of Dubrovnik. A ferry connects them all, as do private boat excursions.

DISTANCE: 17km (10.5 miles)
TIME: A full day
START: Gruž harbour
END: Gruž harbour
POINTS TO NOTE: Scheduled ferries run from Gruž harbour to the Elaphite islands several times a day in summer, but in order to see all three islands it is easier to take one of the excursions that are advertised all over the city. You can opt for one that offers lunch in a Lopud restaurant or a so-called 'fish picnic' on board, or you can be independent and spend your time on the islands as you wish. If you are in Dubrovnik for an extended stay, you could always decide to return later by ferry to the island you liked best.

This archipelago – of which only three islands are inhabited – gives you a relaxing view of rural life. There is not a great deal to do on any of them apart from walking, eating, drinking, swimming and taking in the scenery, but the islands are a tranquil antidote to Dubrovnik in high season.

The journey

Most boat trips start from the harbour at Gruž, from where it is 35–40 minutes to Koločep, the first and smallest of the islands. Look back to land and you will see, above the mouth of the estuary, the striking **Franjo Tuđman Bridge** (named after independent Croatia's first president Franjo Tuđman, who died in 1999), carrying traffic towards Split and Zagreb. As you travel up the coast you will notice how bleak the hillsides are, yellow with broom in early summer but otherwise quite bare and stark. This makes the luxuriant wooded islands, when you reach them, all the more attractive.

A short way out to sea you pass **Daksa**, which belongs to the Elaphite chain but is uninhabited. In the fourteenth century, it was the site of a Franciscan monastery, but it has since achieved a more modern notoriety. In October 1944, the Yugoslav Partisans executed 48 people, including the mayor of Dubrovnik, whom they suspected of sympathising with the Nazis. Their remains weren't

Koločep, one of the Elaphite siblings

discovered until 2009. The current owner of the island has been trying to sell it, so far with no luck.

Koločep

This is the smallest of the inhabited Elaphite Islands, much of it covered in pine forests and with only about 230 people living in the two main settlements. On reaching **Koločep** ❶, boats dock at **Donje Čelo**, a pretty little harbour with terracotta-roofed houses and a narrow strip of sandy beach that is shared by the TUI BLUE Kalamota Island Resort (formerly known as Hotel Villas Koločep). There's also the thirteenth-century Ascension of Mary Church, a few cafés and, at the far end, the Villa Ruža Restaurant in an old stone building, with tables set out beneath pine trees.

If you come here under your own steam, you could take the path through fragrant lemon and orange orchards, pine forests and olive groves to the other little settlement, **Gornje Čelo** ❷. But if you're on an excursion, you won't have time to do much more than walk the length of the harbour, pop into the souvenir shop, and have a quick dip in the sea and a coffee in one of the cafés by the jetty.

If you're staying on Koločep in self-catering accommodation, bear in mind that there are very few places on the island to buy fresh food. Most provisions are delivered from the mainland every morning – including fresh bread, which normally doesn't arrive until mid-morning. It's worth stocking up on as much fresh food as you can carry before boarding the ferry on the mainland.

Šipan

Many boats go next to Šipan, the furthest island (about 45 minutes),

Šipanska Luka at dusk

leaving Lopud as the last stop so that passengers have the most time there for lunch, swimming and exploration. Some trips ignore Šipan altogether, but this is a pity; it is worth taking a tour that includes it, even if for only a brief stop.

Šipan is the largest of the islands but is the least developed for tourism. It was one of the preferred spots for the Dubrovnik aristocracy to build summer residences in the fifteenth century, and there are more than 40 villas and numerous churches scattered across the island. Nowadays, it is more agricultural than the other islands in the chain, and its once-flourishing olive groves and oil production are being revived. However, the population is low – fewer than 500 – and it is hard to imagine young people staying here once they grow up. Scheduled ferries and excursion boats stop at **Suđurađ** ❸ to the southeast, a tiny harbour where houses shelter beneath vines, olives are cultivated on small terraces and gardens are bright with flowers. A little snack bar at the end of the harbour, Stara Mlinica, holds a huge olive press and grinding wheel and has an inviting open hearth that keeps the family warm in winter. If you want a superior lunch, book one of the tables by the harbour at the restaurant at **Hotel Božica** (see ❶).

Two sturdy towers looming up above the harbour belong to the sixteenth-century summer residence

Deer islands

Elaphite means deer, but the deer population on the islands is long gone. There are rumours of wild boar on Šipan, however. Similarly, the human population has dwindled from several thousand to about 850. Lopud alone used to have 4,000; now it's below 300.

of wealthy ship-owner Vice Stjepović-Skočibuha. Approach it from the steps on the other side and you will be able to see down into its cultivated gardens.

If you have time (but you won't if you are on a 'three islands trip'), you could walk to **Šipanska Luka** ❹, the island's other port, about 5km (3 miles) to the northwest. More shadows of Šipan's former glory are dotted about here, including remains of an old duke's palace and what is thought to be a Roman villa. The walk to Šipanska Luka is a pleasant one as you dawdle past olive groves and small vineyards edged with dry-stone walls. The island can get extremely busy in the height of summer with day-trippers, but in temperate months such as September, it's blissfully peaceful.

Lopud

Lopud is the final stop, about 15 minutes later. During the Ragusan Republic this was a thriving port, with a population more than 10 times that

Lunch in sleepy Suđurađ

of today – which is around 230. It produced several Admirals of the Fleet and was the birthplace of ship-owner and merchant Miho Pracat (1528–1607) who, after coming close to financial ruin following two disastrous voyages, finally made a fortune. This he left to the Republic when he died without an heir. There is just one settlement on Lopud now – the little port of the same name built around a sandy bay – but it is increasingly attracting visitors who make it their holiday base, staying in one of the hotels or in the private rooms and apartments you will see on offer. If you enjoy tranquillity, it is a perfect place to stay, especially as no cars are allowed on the island. It is only 55 minutes from Dubrovnik by direct ferry, and ferries run to the island four or five times a day in summer. However, if you are unlucky enough to experience a spell of bad weather, you can feel pretty isolated here as the pace of life on the island is very slow. Out of season, there is even less to do and see.

In the port

Disembarking from the ferry, get your bearings by turning left above the **port** ❺, past the post office to visit the church of **St Mary of Spilica** (Gospa od Spilica). It is attached to a Franciscan monastery established here in 1483, which served as a place of refuge for the islanders as well as performing a religious function. The church has some beautiful paintings and fifteenth-century carved choir stalls, as well as lovely cloisters.

A harbour walk

Back at the harbour, refresh yourself with an ice cream and a cold drink at **Palma** (see ❷). Walk the length of the oleander-lined harbour towards the huge modern RMH Lopud Lafodia Resort see page 93 (www.lafodia hotel.com) at the far end, which has a pool, its own jetty and perfect views of the other islands. En route you will see, beside an imposing but usually closed church, a sign saying Grand Hotel. Venture up the palm-shaded drive through the overgrown gardens and you will find a concrete, modernist building, constructed in 1936 as a sign on the wall informs you, but now deserted and looking decidedly forlorn. There are plans to renovate and reopen the hotel, but funds do not seem to be forthcoming at present. Close by are two tiny chapels, one dedicated to St Jerome, who was born in Dalmatia; the other, the Chapel of the Holy Cross, belonged to Miho Pracat, and his home is believed to have been next door. All that stands there now is a derelict cottage.

You could choose to have lunch in one of the attractive restaurants that line the harbour. **Restoran Dubrovnik** is a friendly place right by the water's edge (see ❸). Wherever you decide to eat, if you're there in high season

Along the Lopud waterfront

you might want to book a table for lunch soon after you arrive rather than waiting for lunchtime when tables fill up rapidly. Little paths lead off the harbour and climb up the hillside, from where you get wonderful views of the coastline and the nearby islands if you take a post-prandial stroll.

Across the island

Afterwards, take the path marked **Plaža Šunj** ❻ beside the Grand Hotel and follow it for about half an hour through pine-scented woods, with conveniently situated benches, to the lovely, sandy Šunj Bay. The water is shallow and safe for children – it's only about knee deep for a good 100 or so metres/yds. There are a couple of summer cafés serving simple food, toilets and showers, and loungers and parasols for hire. There is also an electric golf cart taxi that can transport people with limited mobility for a fee. It's usually waiting at the harbour, so look out for it when you dock.

But don't imagine that it's going to be a secluded spot just because it was a bit of a hike to get here. All excursion boat passengers will have been advised that it's the best beach on the island, and one of the few sandy ones to be found in Croatia's Adriatic coast and islands – something that local people know well. Those who are staying on Lopud have the pleasure of knowing that when the last boat departs for Dubrovnik, the beach will be all theirs.

Food and drink

❶ Hotel Božica
Suđurađ 3, Šipan;
www.hotel-bozica.hr; €€
Locally grown organic produce, including olives and fresh fish, figure prominently on the menu of this classy hotel restaurant. It's in a prime position on a terrace close to Suđurađ's pretty little harbour – all the better to enjoy delicious Ston oysters and wines from the Pelješac peninsula.

❷ Palma
Obala Iva Kuljevana, Lopud;
091-928 0951; €
This busy café overlooking the harbour makes some of the best ice cream you'll find in the region. If you're feeling particularly hungry, try one of their giant stacked ice-cream desserts.

❸ Restoran Dubrovnik
Obala Iva Kuljevana 40, Lopud;
www.restaurantdubrovnik-lopud.com;
€€–€€€
Right by the water's edge at the harbour is this relaxed, family-run restaurant serving good-quality seafood and Dalmatian meat dishes. It's worth booking in advance during the summer, even by only a few hours.

TOUR 8
Mljet

Mljet is a beautiful island to the northwest of Dubrovnik. It makes a delightful day out from the city, but there is accommodation if you want to stay longer.

> **DISTANCE:** 10km (6.2 miles)
> **TIME:** A full day
> **START:** Polače harbour, Mljet
> **END:** Polače harbour
> **POINTS TO NOTE:** The catamaran *Nona Ana* leaves Gruž harbour and takes about 90 minutes to reach Polače. It's best to buy tickets online in advance, especially during high season. Tickets are also available at the small white kiosk across the road from the Jadrolinija ferry office. If you're spending just one day on Mljet, make sure you get off at the second port, Polače, not at Sobra on the eastern end of the island. Take swimming gear and a picnic if you don't want to eat at one of the restaurants. Several agencies run excursions to Mljet for an all-in price, with a guide, but getting there under your own steam is not difficult.

Unlike the bare mainland coastline, Mljet (pronounced *Mlyet*) is richly forested and offers much welcome shade on a hot day. Unspoilt, wild and beautiful, it covers roughly 100 sq km (38 sq miles); the western end, where the catamaran will dock, is a national park established in 1960. Its area of 31 sq km (12 sq miles) encompasses several small settlements, the port of Pomena, as well as the lakes and surrounding terrain.

Polače

Polače's ❶ ruined Roman walls give little clue that a palace second in size only to Diocletian's in Split had stood here – hence the name Polače. Even during the height of the season, the place remains a sleepy Adriatic fishing village. Its large bay is sheltered by four islets, Tajnik, Moračnik, Ovrata and Kobrava. There are a few small restaurants here, but you might want to save yourself for lunch in Pomena if you don't bring your own food.

National park

To get to **Mljet National Park** ❷ (http://np-mljet.hr), you can hire a bike opposite the jetty at Polače, or a beach buggy or scooter from Mini Brum 100 metres/yds to the left

A third of Mljet is protected as a national park

(www.rent-a-car-scooter-mljet.hr), but most people head for the park kiosk just to the right. Here you pay your entrance fee, which includes minibus transport to and from the park, and the boat fare out to Sveta Marija (St Mary's Island). The fee may seem a bit steep, but all the profits are ploughed back into the upkeep of the park.

St Mary's island

A five-minute bus ride takes you to **Pristanište** ❸ on the shore of **Veliko Jezero** (Big Lake), actually a tidal expanse of saltwater, fed by the sea. Here you can board a small boat to the island of **Sveta Marija** ❹ (St Mary). The Benedictine monastery and church here have a chequered architectural history. The church and parts of the monastery are Romanesque and date from the twelfth century, but additions were made in the fourteenth century, and it was extended further during the subsequent two centuries, when it was given a Renaissance façade. After the monks abandoned the place in 1808, it fell into disrepair and is now being renovated by the St Mary's Foundation, in conjunction with the Diocese of Dubrovnik, to which it was handed back in 1997 under the Law of Returned Property. The church, an imposing single-naved structure, is coming along nicely and can be visited, but the monastery and cloister are still under wraps and closed to visitors. However, the ground floor functions as the Restaurant Melita, right on the water's edge. The food can be disappointing but the setting is beautiful.

Wander along the shady island paths, which won't take more than 15 minutes, even if you stop to visit the two little votive chapels, built by grateful sailors who had survived watery misfortunes. If you've brought your swimming gear, take a dip off the rocks and dry out in the sun before getting the boat back to shore. The trip will not go directly to your starting point, but will take you to Mali Most (Small Bridge) on the edge of **Malo Jezero** ❺ (Small Lake). Here there's a small swimming beach and opportunities to rent kayaks, canoes and rowing boats.

Pomena

A path marked 'Pomena' – all the park's paths are clearly signposted – takes you round the side of Malo Jezero along on a pleasant route, easy underfoot, bordered by pines and olive trees. After a while the path leaves the lake and goes up a fairly gentle wooded hill, then descends to the little settlement of **Pomena** ❻. Once a tiny fishing village, it is now Mljet's tourist centre – but a restrained and pretty one. The Hotel Odisej dominates the bay. The name (Odyssey) relates to the popular myth that Ulysses stopped on Mljet during his voyage – one of several southern European countries to lay the same claim. Some

Polače harbour restaurant

smart yachts bob in the little bay, and there are several good restaurants.

Follow a path round to the right of the harbour to find a row of little eating places. Lobster is advertised at many restaurants on the island but, as everywhere else, it is expensive and is usually priced by the kilo. There's plenty of other seafood, though, and at good prices, and Pomena would make a delightful lunch stop if you didn't eat on the island. **Barba Ive** (see ❶) is a good bet. There are more opportunities to rent buggies here from Mini Brum, many of them painted to resemble tigers, zebras or monkeys, and bikes can be hired from the hotel.

Back to the boat

When you are ready to head back the 2.5km (1.5 miles) to Pristanište to pick up the minibus, retrace your steps as far as Mali Most and continue along the lake shore. You will pass a pretty settlement, **Babine Kuće** ❼, where there is another opportunity

Pine groves provide much-needed shade

to eat or drink at **Mali Raj** (see ❷), on a geranium-clad terrace beneath a vine. Don't linger too long, as there's only one boat back. If you have time and can't resist the lure of the lakes, you can pass the pick-up point and clamber down to the water's edge for another swim. As long as there are no signs prohibiting swimming, and you are not near the seaward exit from the lake where the current is strong, you may swim anywhere.

Back in Polače, you could wander around the ruined walls of the Roman palace, but this won't detain you for long. Better to sit in one of the cafés that line the waterfront, enjoy the smell of wood smoke as restaurateurs fire up their barbecues, and sample the local dessert wine, *prošek*, while you wait for boarding time.

If you plan to stay for more than a day, there is a wealth of trails to explore in the park, none of them too taxing, although there are a few steep gradients. You can buy a map with marked trails from one of the official kiosks. There are also several sandy beaches to visit on the eastern side of the island. Check Mljet's tourist board (www.mljet.hr) for accommodation. You'll also need to consider transport. The public bus service is patchy at best. Buses connect the two ferry ports, but they're on a limited schedule and unreliable. Car hire is easy to arrange in the main villages, and hiring a scooter is easier, cheaper and often more practical. If you just get so carried away with the island that you miss the boat back to Dubrovnik, you will have to knock on one of the doors advertising a *soba* – a room for rent.

Eastern Mljet

Visitors planning to spend more time on Mljet can take the ferry from Dubrovnik to **Sobra** ❽, the main port on the eastern side of the island. Ferries run all year round to this little fishing village of stone houses in a sheltered bay backed by steep hills. There's no beach, but that doesn't stop people from swimming off the rocks. There are a few restaurants and a market, as well as a handful of guesthouses, rooms to rent and self-catering apartments, some of which are set on the hillside with lovely sea views. It's sleepy, relaxed and pleasantly slow.

About 6km (4 miles) from Sobra is **Babino Polje** ❾, one of the island's oldest villages. It sits in the shadow of the island's highest peak, Veliki Grad (514 metres/1,686ft), while below are the fertile fields that give the village its name. Veliki Grad is also on a well-marked hiking trail that starts in Pomena, curves up to Polače and eventually snakes across the island for 40km (25 miles) to Sobra. The views from Veliki Grad stretch as far as the mainland and neighbouring islands, and are worth the hike up the scrubby hillside. Babino Polje is actually three hamlets – Zadublje, Srčenovići and

St Mary's Island

Ulysses Cave

Food and drink

① Barba Ive
Pomena 4; 098-669 662; €€–€€€
For fish so fresh it still twitches, head to this friendly waterfront restaurant for beautifully cooked dishes including octopus stew and seafood risotto. Meat-eaters are catered for too, with plenty of Dalmatian specialities including *pršut*.

② Mali Raj
Babine Kuće 3; www.maliraj-mljet.com; €€
This is a lovely spot to stop and have a cold drink before heading back to Polače to catch the catamaran back to Dubrovnik. Or if you have time for lunch, try the grilled squid. It also offers three apartments to rent.

③ Kod Ante
Saplunara; www.pinetreemljet.com; €€–€€€
Overlooking Saplunara Bay is the friendly restaurant that's part of the immensely stylish PineTree Boutique Apartments. Order ahead to have one of its dishes cooked under a *peka*, or go for the lobster spaghetti.

Zabriježe – of old stone houses clustered together. There are several campsites in the area, as is **Sutmiholjska**, a soft pebbly beach tucked into a narrow cove a few kilometres away on the southern coast. The pine groves backing the beach offer some wonderful shade on a hot day. Facilities are minimal, so you might want to bring your own supplies.

Not far from Sutmiholjska beach is Ulysses Cave – one of many caves along this limestone karst coast, although this one is said to have sheltered Ulysses on his lengthy odyssey. Fearless locals make use of the raised shoreline around the cave and jump straight into the sparkling blue water and swim into the grotto. There are lower points from which to jump if you're not quite so brave.

For a country where sandy beaches are rare, it's unusual to find three very close to each other – and on a relatively small island. At Mljet's southernmost point is an oddly shaped peninsula, into which one of its many indents is **Limuni** beach (also called Uvala Blaće). Fingers of pine forests arc protectively around the beach of fine sand, which has a long shallow section of clear blue-green water. It can be reached by road, even if the last part of it isn't paved.

Slightly more accessible is its near neighbour, **Saplunara** ⑩. You won't find many facilities here, but you will find Aleppo pines and two beaches of soft sand. There's also a shingle beach closer to the centre. The village itself is very small (population approximately 83), but it does offer a few guesthouses and private rooms. **Kod Ante** (see page 93), overlooking the beach, serves locally sourced food (see ③).

Sunbathing near the canal entrance to Veliko Jezero, Big Lake

TOUR 9
Cavtat

Take the boat from Dubrovnik's Old Port to this pretty village where restaurants line the quayside and a pleasant wooded path circles the peninsula.

> **DISTANCE:** 3km (1.8 miles)
> **TIME:** Half a day
> **START:** Cavtat Harbour
> **END:** Cavtat Harbour
> **POINTS TO NOTE:** In summer, boats leave Dubrovnik's Old Port for Cavtat throughout the day. The regular service takes about 45 minutes, but some boats stop at points along the coast and take longer – check when you book. The last boat back from Cavtat is usually about 5.30pm but may vary depending on the time of year. There is also a bus service (No. 10), which is a good choice – and much cheaper – if the sea is rough.

Cavtat is an attractive village about 17km (10.5 miles) south of Dubrovnik, on a peninsula between two bays. It was the site of first a Greek, then a Roman settlement of Epidaurus and the place from which the Illyrian inhabitants fled in the seventh century to found Ragusa. The foundations of a fort on the tip of the peninsula are all that remain of the Roman period.

A visit to Cavtat (pronounced *Tsavtat*) is one of the most popular day trips from Dubrovnik. Its proximity to the airport makes it a good option if you have an early flight, but the village is also an appealing destination in its own right, with a relaxed atmosphere and good restaurants and cafés. Many visitors prefer to base themselves in Cavtat and take the boat or bus into Dubrovnik. Although the boats stop running relatively early, the buses carry on all evening, giving you the chance to experience a different side of Dubrovnik in the evening once the crowds have gone back to their cruise ships.

During July and August, Cavtat holds many events during its summer festival, including concerts with choirs and folklore groups, as well as water polo tournaments. In September, it's time for the Epidaurus Festival, a celebration of classical music and the arts in general. And in February, the town puts on its own pre-Lenten carnival.

As your boat approaches the harbour, you will have a picture-postcard view of a palm-lined promenade with a church at either

Honey-stoned Cavtat

end, and inviting restaurants and cafés in between. Depending on the time of day, you might even catch some water polo teams practising in one cordoned-off area of the port.

To the right, as you disembark, is the parish church of **St Nicholas** ❶ (Svetog Nikole). Next door, the former Rector's Palace is now the **Baltazar Bogišić Collection** ❷, housing the library and paintings, costumes and other items collected by Vlaho Bogišić, a writer and lawyer born here in 1834,

whose bulky statue sits opposite. Beside him is a triangle of restaurants, of which the best known is **Leut** (see ❶).

Monastery and Mausoleum

Return along the harbourfront, picking your way between restaurant tables, past the attractive Hotel Supetar, to reach the **Franciscan Monastery Church** ❸ (Franjevački Samostan Crkva; free). The eye-catching polyptych of St Michael (1510) to the left of the door is the work of Vicko Dobričević, son of Lovro

Cavtat's rooftops and mountainous interior

(see walk 1). One oddity in this plain and peaceful little church (although it is not uncommon in Croatia) is a disembodied hand appearing from the pulpit, holding a crucifix.

Behind the church, turn left into Ulica Kvaternikova, then continue up a flight of steps to the hilltop cemetery, dominated by the **Račić Family Mausoleum** ❹. This octagonal, white marble structure was designed in 1922 by Ivan Meštrović, the best-known twentieth-century Croatian sculptor, for the super-wealthy ship-owning family. Its bronze doors, with images of four Slav saints, are guarded by a pair of Art Nouveau-style angels, while another angel flexes his wings on the cupola. The Račićs, who followed each other to the mausoleum in quick succession in the 1920s, obviously wanted to appear as opulent in death as they were in life.

Around the peninsula

After admiring the sweeping coastal views, leave the cemetery by the back gate and follow a sloping path through pine woods. Where the path divides, you could take the right fork and follow it around the outside of town, to arrive back at the church of St Nicholas. Better, though, to take the steps down to a bathing area, where there's a beach café and sun loungers and umbrellas to rent in summer. Here a concreted path continues along the waterside to Cavtat's second bay, Uvala Tiha. This is the pick-up and drop-off point for coaches and public buses.

The road parallel to the bay, past the police station and a small branch of the tourist office, soon becomes quieter, more rural, and is lined with cypresses. The road then widens out again when it reaches the Remisens Hotel Albatros. A short distance further along, at the Remisens Hotel Epidaurus, the path peters out altogether.

Another option would be to bypass the walk up to the cemetery and take a gentle stroll under umbrella pines around the 7km (4.3-mile) smooth shaded path that hugs the peninsula.

A detour

Those with more time and energy may like to try the Ronald Brown Pathway, which starts behind the Hotel Albatros and leads to a cross on a hilltop. This marks the spot where the plane carrying the US Secretary of Commerce and the rest of a trade delegation to Croatia crashed in 1996. The trail takes at least two hours, and winds steeply uphill. The narrowness and terrain of the path make it unsuitable when bad weather strikes, as clouds can descend very quickly. Anyone walking the trail would be advised to wear proper footwear.

Bukovac's gallery

Now return to the harbour for lunch, if you haven't already done so. Once you're ready to move on, take the fifth little lane on your right from the promenade,

Food and drink

● Leut
Trumbićev put 17;
www.restaurant-leut.com; €€–€€€
Leut has been run by the same family since 1971. Its waterside location is a beautiful backdrop to seafood dishes that are rich in lobster and prawns. Reservations are advisable for weekends and in high season, especially for Sunday lunch.

Ulica Bukovčeva, to visit **Bukovac House** ❺, dedicated to Vlaho Bukovac (1855–1922), the highly esteemed and prolific artist who was born here. Bukovac had a hard life as a young man, but was accepted by the Paris École des Beaux-Arts after gaining the financial backing of the enlightened Bishop Strossmayer. The artist worked for many years in Zagreb before becoming a professor at the Prague Academy.

The ground floor of the house is empty except for some modern paintings, but the walls and staircases throughout are colour-washed and decorated with friezes depicting birds, animals and rural scenes – all by Bukovac. Upstairs, two large rooms display many of his portraits, mostly of family members – detailed, contemplative and memorable. One chilling picture, in a room by itself, apparently shows the heads of the artist and his wife lying on a table, looking up at those of four children, suspended by their hair.

After, pause for a coffee on the seafront while you wait for your boat. A word of warning: if the sea gets really choppy, the smaller boats will not make the journey, so you will have to go back by bus. This is no great hardship: bus No.10 runs regularly from the terminal in Tiha Bay, where a timetable is posted, to Dubrovnik bus station, with stops en route. The journey takes about half an hour.

The region south of Cavtat, down to Montenegro, is Konavle, a rich agricultural district where the silk moth is cultivated. This silk is used in local costumes worn at the Sunday folk gatherings in the village of Čilipi near the airport. Hillside hamlets make up Pridvorje, a town eulogised by Dubrovnik's Renaissance poets. Now a series of hamlets, the community includes a Franciscan monastery and a former palace of the rector of Konavle. If you don't have your own transport, the region can be explored in various ways including a Jeep safari, an organised food and folklore tour, a guided jaunt on a quad bike or a ride on a scenic tourist train through the vineyards. Bicycle hire is easy to arrange in Cavtat, which is the starting point for a 9.5km (6 miles) route to Čilipi. The village is now home to the **Konavle County Museum** (www.migk.hr; charge) with a rich collection of folk costumes, textiles and embroideries.

Waterfront restaurants in Cavtat

TOUR 10
Trsteno and Ston

Take a trip up the coast to visit one of Croatia's oldest botanical gardens, and onwards to the twin villages of Ston and Mali Ston to sample some of the best oysters in the country.

DISTANCE: 55km (34 miles) by car each way
TIME: A full day
START: Dubrovnik
END: Dubrovnik
POINTS TO NOTE: It would be best to hire a car for this trip, as buses to Ston are infrequent, and you might like to combine it with a stay in Korčula (see walk 11). If you just want to visit Trsteno, the bus to Split which leaves approximately every hour from the long-distance bus station at Gruž harbour will drop you off there, and will also stop at Zaton.

Trsteno is a miniscule village located around 18km (11 miles) up the coast from Dubrovnik which has gained a wide reputation for its ethereal Arboretum. The scenic car journey here runs along a beautiful stretch of coast with sweeping views across a number of islands, including Mljet in the distance and the cragged Elaphite Islands.

The twin villages of Ston and Mali Ston on the Pelješac peninsula are known principally for having some of the best oysters in the world and for their huge defensive walls, claimed to be second only to the Great Wall of China.

Seaside stop in Zaton

If you are driving, follow signs to Split, which take you up above the town and across the Tuđman Bridge. From there it's a pleasant 10km (6.2-mile) drive to **Zaton** ❶, set in a deep bay that causes the highway to scuttle inland around farmland. Zaton is divided in two: Veliki (Large) and Mali (Small), and together they form an attractive little settlement that is building up its tourist infrastructure, catering to those who want to be outside Dubrovnik but within easy reach of the city. There are a number of residences that were once the summer retreats of wealthy families. If you're here around lunchtime, stop at **Restaurant Gverović-Orsan** (see ❶), set in an old boathouse, after which it is named.

Arboretum fountain, Trsteno

Trsteno Arboretum

Some 8km (5 miles) further on you reach **Trsteno**, where two huge 500-year-old plane trees dominate the main street. You can't miss them: their diameters are about 5 metres (16ft). Turn left beside the trees down a narrow road and you will shortly reach the **Arboretum** ❷ (www.pvdp.hr/en/home), which now belongs to the Croatian Academy of Science and the Arts.

Established as a summer residence and garden in the late fifteenth century by Ivan Gučetić, a prominent member of Ragusa's nobility, it has changed and expanded over the years and now sprawls across an area of 25 hectares (63 acres). The collection includes more than 300 species of trees, shrubs and plants, some rare and exotic, in a delightful setting running down to the sea. This makes a lovely, shady place to spend some time on a hot summer's day. Fans of the *Game of Thrones* television series will certainly recognise the setting as the King's Landing palace gardens.

Towards the end of 1991, the Arboretum came under a dual attack from sea and air, and much of it was destroyed in the subsequent fire,

Picturesque Trsteno harbour

the café at the garden's entrance and leave your car in the café's car park.

Ston

Follow the coast for another 30km (18 miles) or so and you will come to **Ston** ❸, which, like Zaton, is divided in two. The larger village is sometimes called Veliki (Large) Ston, and the smaller is always known as Mali (Little) Ston. They sit at the head of the Pelješac peninsula, divided by a narrow isthmus. The 5km (3 miles) of great walls that connect the two (and for which World Heritage status is being sought) were built in the fourteenth century, principally to protect the salt pans, which you will see as you drive between the two settlements. Still in use today (you can buy little cloth bags of Ston salt, which make a nice souvenir), the salt pans were once vital to Ragusa's economy and were much coveted by Napoleon. The energetic can climb the walls from Veliki Ston for fabulous views of the salt pans and the surrounding area.

You reach Mali Ston first, but save this for later and turn left instead, and drive about 2km (1.2 miles) to Ston. The Veliki is a misnomer: although it's called a town, and it has a long history, having been founded in 1333, it is not much more than a village, with a population of about 500. Ston has little to offer in the way of sites or entertainment, but it's an appealing

although the oldest part escaped without too much damage. A great deal of restoration has been done since then, and the garden, a mixture of formal and semi-wild areas, is delightful – as is the over-the-top, eighteenth-century Neptune's Grotto, with dolphin fountains and water lilies. If you are driving, park in the designated area and you will see nearby a sign pointing towards a little beach to which you can make your way if you feel like a swim after you have explored the garden. As parking can be difficult at peak times, you might want to have a drink at

Food and drink

① Restaurant Gverović-Orsan
Na Ratu 7, Zaton Mali;
www.gverovic-orsan.hr; €€–€€€
Savour squid-ink risotto and prawn gnocchi in a peaceful location right by the water's edge, where you can have a swim afterwards. This is an appealing option for lunch even if you return to Dubrovnik immediately afterwards, so it's best to book ahead during the season.

② Kapetanova Kuća
Obala Dr Ante Starčevića, Mali Ston;
www.ostrea.hr; €€–€€€
This waterside restaurant gets busy in the summer, so book ahead to enjoy Ston oysters and fresh seafood as well as excellent wines from wineries in the Pelješac peninsula.

---

and friendly little place with several churches and a morning market.

The café tables set out in the central square, shaded by lime trees and flowering shrubs, make it a good place to stop for coffee. The area was badly hit by an earthquake in 1996 (fortunately with no loss of life), and there are hardly any signs of damage to be seen.

Oyster central

Return now to Mali Ston, which is tiny, just a cluster of houses around a fortified tower, set beside a bay that gives the place its *raison d'être* – oysters.

In 1936, the General Trades International Exhibition awarded these oysters the Grand Prix, declaring them the best in the world. You will have seen the expanses of oyster beds as you approach the village. The best-known restaurant in which to sample the molluscs, the Villa Koruna (see page 103), displays a certificate awarded at the 1936 exhibition. That seems a very long time ago, and many things have changed since then, but the oysters – and the mussels – still rank among the best and bring flocks of people here for Sunday lunch.

And lunch is what you will probably be interested in as well. If the Koruna – with its huge tanks of fish and a couple of slowly circling turtles – is busy with tour groups, as it sometimes is, walk round to the left of the restaurant, past the great tower. Here you will find **Bota Šare** (see page 103) and **Kapetanova Kuća** (see ②), both of which offer excellent seafood at tables right beside the bay.

If you don't like oysters, don't worry, there's plenty more to choose from: garlicky mussels, black risotto (made with squid ink) and lobster soup, to mention just a few.

Mali Ston fisherman

WALK 11
Korčula

This fertile island northwest of Dubrovnik is a destination in its own right, but can be visited in a day in this excursion that concentrates on the walled town of Korčula itself.

> **DISTANCE:** 1.5km (0.9 miles)
> **TIME:** A full day
> **START:** Korčula harbour
> **END:** Korčula harbour
> **POINTS TO NOTE:** You can get to the island by ferry (about 3.5 hours) or by faster catamaran if you go on an organised excursion. But if you come in winter, or would like to spend more than a few hours here, you could hire a car, drive the 115km (70 miles) then make the 15-minute ferry crossing from Orebić, from where boats do operate in winter. You could then spend the night here and perhaps combine the trip with a visit to Ston and Trsteno en route or on the following day.

Korčula, which is 48 nautical miles northwest of Dubrovnik, is lush and bountiful. Like the Pelješac peninsula from which it is separated by a narrow channel, it specialises in wine. This area produces some of the best wine in Croatia, but most of it is for domestic consumption. The finest beaches are on the south of the island, and are worth exploring if you are here on an extended stay.

Getting to the island

Shortly after the town of Prizdrina the vineyards peter out, the landscape becomes barer and rockier, and ahead you see the glittering sea, framing the island of Korčula. The port of Orebić, from where you take the ferry, is small, but to the north are some of the coast's best sandy beaches, popular with windsurfers. There are car ferries from here, but if you plan to concentrate on the town of Korčula, as this itinerary does, it would be as well to leave your car here and take the passenger ferry across. The Old Town itself is pedestrianised, and outlying areas are easily reached on foot or bus. As your boat takes you across the narrow channel, the walled town, with its four sturdy towers, honey-coloured walls and terracotta roofs, resembles a fairy-tale city.

Once in the harbour (don't forget to check on return boat times), you will see a broad flight of steps, dividing around a central fountain. This is

Walled Korčula Town

Primorska Vrata ❶ (Sea Gate), one of two entrances to the Old Town. Adjacent, the tourist office is set in a splendid sixteenth-century loggia. If you are going to stay the night on the island, the elegant Aminess Korčula Heritage Hotel (see page 93) next door is a good choice.

The Old Town

At the top of the steps, a broad terrace is lined with café tables and, straight ahead, a narrow alley (Ulica Dinka Miroševiča) leads up to **St Mark's Square** where you will find the Cathedral, the Treasury Museum and the Town Museum. The Gothic-Renaissance **St Mark's Cathedral** ❷ (Katedrala Sveti Marka) is constructed, like most of Korčula's buildings, from the mellow limestone that made the island – and its stone masters – prosperous and famous. The tower and cupola, dating from around 1480, are the work of Marko Andrijić, whose sons, Petar and Josip, worked on many

St Mark's Cathedral

prestigious buildings in Dubrovnik. Flanking the main doorway are lions and some naked figures representing Adam and Eve. Above the door sits St Mark, robed as a bishop. Inside, the Cathedral is notable for a splendid, high wooden ceiling; a huge stone canopy, also the work of Andrijić père, and built to his own design; and a richly coloured Tintoretto altarpiece (1550) depicting St Mark flanked by St Bartholomew and St Jerome. In the south aisle there is an Annunciation that is ascribed to the School of Tintoretto; and in the north aisle is Ivan Meštrović's early twentieth-century bronze statue of St Blaise.

To the right of the Cathedral is the **Treasury Museum** ❸ (Opatska Riznica). Inside, its eclectic array of artworks range from fifteenth-century sacred paintings – including a precious polyptych of *Our Lady of Conception* by Blaž Trogiranin, one of the most respected fifteenth-century Dalmatian artists – to Ivan Meštrović's twentieth-century bronze *Pietà*. There are also ecclesiastical robes, chalices and processional crucifixes; and at ground level there's a cool kitchen, whose shelves are stacked with Roman pots and jars of all shapes and sizes, recovered from the sea in the 1960s.

Opposite, the **Town Museum** ❹ (Gradski Muzej; https://gradskimuzej-korcula.hr/hr; charge), in a sixteenth-century Renaissance palace built for the wealthy Gabrielis family, showcases an interesting exhibition on the island's stonemasons. It also focuses on Korčula's other important industry – shipbuilding – which utilised timber from the densely wooded island. At their height, the shipyards rivalled those of Venice and Dubrovnik; at the end of the eighteenth century there were still 100 shipyards here. Elsewhere, rooms house seventeenth- to nineteenth-century furniture, elaborate costumes, portraits of the Andrijić family, kitchen implements and, easily overlooked, photographs of Tito's Partisans.

If you are hungry there are plenty of places to sit down and eat. Korčula's restaurants offer the usual selection of seafood and Dalmatian ham, but they also specialise in pizza. Try **Buffet-Pizzeria Amfora** south of the Cathedral in Ulica od Teatra (see ❶). For something fishy, go to **Konoba Adio Mare** (see ❷), a short way down Ulica Sveti Roka. Another of the island's specialities – sea urchin eggs – may prove more difficult to find, unless you know a local fisherman.

The Marco Polo connection

It is generally agreed that Marco Polo (1254–1324) was born in Venice, but, as you will soon discover, that is not accepted on this island. Korčula claims the great explorer for its own, believing that he was born here before his family moved to the Italian city of canals. There is a Hotel Marco Polo (on the next peninsula, east of the Old Town), and Marco Polo Tours operates close to

Cannon guarding the waterfront

Tintoretto altarpiece

the harbour. The **Marco Polo Tower** ❺ in Ulica Depolo, off Ulica Sveti Roka, is reputedly where he was born.

Korčula is known for its festivals and its desire to keep traditions alive. The most important celebration is the Moreška, or Sword Dance Festival, held on St Theodor's Day, 29 July, when lavishly dressed medieval knights perform a stylised dance and play, similar to the Moors and Christians festivals in Spain. A shortened version of the dance takes place on an outdoor stage in the Ljetno Kino every week in summer.

Icons and ice cream

Leave Marco Polo behind now, and, bypassing the Cathedral, follow the road called Ulica Korčulanskog Statuta 1214. The cumbersome name relates to the City Statute of 1214, one of the oldest Slav legal documents, which laid down the rights and obligations of citizens and regulated trade and agriculture. At the end of the road (only a few hundred metres), turn left into Ulica Kaporova to visit **All Saints' Church** ❻ (Svih Svetih; free) to see a beautiful fifteenth-century polyptych by Blaž Trogiranin (whose work is also in the Treasury Museum). Next door is the **Icon Museum** ❼ (Zhirka Ikona), housed in the Hall of the Brotherhood of All Saints. Painted on wood in tempera and gilt, some of the icons are truly moving.

From here, you could follow the broad, pine-shaded road (Petra Kanavelića) that leads back around the town in an anti-clockwise direction, stopping for an ice cream at one of the cafés. Alternatively, backtrack to the main road, where it opens out into a small square, with the **Gradska Vijećnica** ❽ (Town Hall) on the right and, on the left, the fifteenth-century **Veliko Revelin** ❾ (Large Tower), which guards the **Kopnena Vrata** ❿ (Land Gate) to the town.

Outside the walls

After climbing the tower for far-reaching views of the glistening sea and the coastline, you could go down the steps out of the Old Town and turn right, walking a few metres until you reach the great, cone-shaped **Velika Kneževa Kula** ⓫ (Large Governor's Tower), built at the western corner of the walls to protect both the Governor's Palace and the harbour. Turn left here, and follow the harbour road for a different view of Korčula and the chance for a swim at one of two small bathing beaches. If you want to check out the Marina, or are going to stay in one of the hotels on the next little peninsula east, go left when you come out of the Land Gate and follow the road round to the right. Here you'll find opportunities for swimming and sailing (Korčula's a truly great place for sailing and hosts a number of regattas) as well as just sitting by the sea, resting your feet and watching the boats in the water.

For one of the quirkiest spots for a

Kopnena Vrata (Land Gate)

sundowner, head to the northern tip of the Old Town until you see the hulking fifteenth-century Zakerjan tower, now home to **Cocktail Bar Massimo** (see ❸). Climb the steep ladder in the turret until you reach the open-air terrace at the top – one of the loveliest places to watch the sun go down over a cocktail.

Further afield

If you plan to stay longer in Korčula and explore some of its beaches, it's about a 15-minute bus ride to the small fishing village of **Lumbarda**. Here among the vineyards you'll find several sandy stretches, including the small village beach at the bottom of the harbour. The larger Vela Pržina is tucked into a cove on the southern side of the island. It's popular, so arrive early. Closer to Lumbarda is the equally busy beach at Bilin Žal, which is also connected by bus to Korčula Town as well as taxi boat. Lumbarda produces some of Korčula's best wine, including dry white Grk which is cultivated solely in Lumbarda's six wineries.

Visit **Bire Winery** (www.bire.hr) or **Zure Wines** (www.zure.hr) for a tasting, and enjoy lunch or dinner at Zure's vine-covered restaurant.

The beach is a favourite spot for sailors to stop for a swim while on excursions around the **Skoji islands** directly to the north. This archipelago of nineteen islands can be visited easily on day trips from Lumbarda and Korčula Town, and provide an enjoyable escape from the crowds that can descend in high season. Trips to the Skoji islands can include discovering hidden beaches, snorkelling, diving, canoeing and kayaking, as well as picnics on the boat. The largest of the islands, **Badija**, is home to a Franciscan monastery, pebbly beaches and an attractive beachfront café.

Food and drink

❶ Buffet-Pizzeria Amfora
Ulica od Teatra 4; 099-818 4835; €
Choose between large pizzas, simply grilled fish and good-quality pasta and seafood dishes in an attractive narrow lane a few streets south of the Cathedral.

❷ Konobia Adio Mare
Ulica Sveti Roka 2; www.konobaadiomare.hr; €€–€€€
Try to get a table on the roof terrace of this atmospheric restaurant with an extensive fish and seafood menu including grilled fish and squid. It's worth booking during high season.

❸ Cocktail Bar Massimo
Šetalište Petra Kanavelića; 099-214 4568; €€
Half the fun is getting to the top of the medieval tower before settling down with a cocktail and taking in glorious views.

Badija island, off Korčula

DIRECTORY

Our edit of the best hotels, restaurants and evening entertainment to suit all tastes and budgets, plus an A–Z of all the essential information you need to know, a quick language guide, and some great book and film recommendations to give you a flavour of the city.

Accommodation	**86**
Restaurants	**94**
Nightlife	**104**
Essentials	**106**
Language	**116**
Books and film	**120**
About this book	**122**

Accommodation

Many of Dubrovnik's hotels are spacious, modern and efficient, with air conditioning, swimming pools, room service, etc. A large number has been swallowed up by a small number of conglomerates such as Adriatic Luxury Hotels and Valamar. Many visitors to Dubrovnik come on package deals, which usually include half-board accommodation, generally at a price considerably lower than the rack rates given below.

There are a few smaller, more personal hotels, however, and a growing number of rooms and apartments for rent – look for signs saying *sobe* or *apartman*. The identical dark blue signs indicate that the establishment is regulated. A room in a private house usually doesn't include breakfast, so you have to go to the nearest café.

All hotel rates vary according to the time of year – there are some very good deals to be had off-season, although many close over the winter. The rates below are for a standard, en-suite double room in high season (July–mid-September) including breakfast.

Old Town

l'Amoret Apartments
4 locations; www.dubrovnik-amoret.com
Choose from 15 apartments set in four former palaces near the cathedral, all furnished with antiques and family heirlooms. The one-bedroom flat has a full kitchen, but if you don't plan to cook much, the studio flats with small kitchenettes are more affordable. €€€

The Byron
Pobijana 4; www.thebyrondubrovnik.com
Between the Cathedral and the City Walls is this beautifully furnished boutique hotel run by the same couple who used to run the (now closed) Fresh Sheets B&B. There are only seven rooms, six of which come with kitchenettes. €€€€

Karmen Apartments
Bandureva 1; www.karmendu.com
These three spacious (and one smaller) apartments are in a family house right beside the harbour. They're attractively decorated, with bright rugs and bedspreads, original paintings on the walls and smart, modern bathrooms. The friendly, helpful hosts

> **Price categories**
> Price guide for a double room in high season including breakfast:
> €€€€ = over €375
> €€€ = €175–375
> €€ = €90–175
> € = under 90

Sleep in style at Stari Grad

have loads of local knowledge that they are happy to share. €€–€€€

Prijeko Palace
Prijeko 22; www.prijekopalace.com
Contemporary artists have been let loose on the nine luxurious rooms in this sixteenth-century house in Prijeko, and furnished them with original works. The result is a riot of colour and a sumptuous baroque style that's a world away from modern minimalism. Head to the roof terrace for fantastic views of the Old Town. €€€€

Pucić Palace
Od Puča 1; www.thepucicpalace.com
Set in a Renaissance palace, Pucić Palace offers 19 rooms and suites. There's a restaurant, a brasserie, a beauty centre and a library in an old chapel. The hotel also has sunbeds and umbrellas reserved for guests on Banje Beach. €€€€

Scalini Palace
Boškovićeva 3; www.scalinipalace.com
Book ahead to get one of the three elegant suites in this sixteenth-century stone townhouse just off Stradun. All have full kitchens, and one has a balcony for alfresco meals. €€€–€€€€

St Joseph's
Svetog Josipa 3; www.stjosephs.hr
This romantic and intimate boutique hotel is located in a 500-year-old house tucked away in a quiet lane off Stradun. Its six sumptuous rooms

Pucić Palace

are decorated in a refined yet relaxed French country cottage style and come with kitchenettes and modern marble bathrooms. A few doors down is St Joseph's Cottage, where three additional rooms share a kitchen. €€€€

Stari Grad
Od Sigurate 4; www.hotelstarigrad.com
This 11-room boutique hotel occupies an aristocratic family house just off Stradun. Smartly furnished modern rooms have contemporary decor, and the rooftop terrace restaurant, Above 5, has wonderful views of the Old Town. Treat yourself to a session in the Icona Thai Spa. €€€€

Villa Ragusa
Žudioska 15; www.villaragusadubrovnik.com

Stari Grad's smartly decorated rooms

It's a bit of a climb to reach this 600-year-old building, but it's worth it if you want a comfortable, reasonably priced option. There's a nicely rustic room on each of the five floors, with a shared kitchen and dining area. The whole house is also available to rent. €€–€€€

Ploče

Casa Bianca
Frana Supila 39; https://casabianca-dubrovnik.com
Choose from four contemporary apartments in this sleek modern building above Villa Sheherezade. There's a one-bedroom, a two-bed and two three-beds, all with quietly luxurious furnishings, terraces and floor-length windows. Three of the four have full sea views, while the fourth has partial sea views. €€€–€€€€

Hotel Excelsior
Frana Supila 12; www.adriaticluxuryhotels.com
About five minutes' walk from the Ploče Gate is this large five-star hotel with splendid views of the old town. The hotel dates from 1913 and there's a 1970s extension, both with contemporary interior, along with a swimming platform, an indoor pool and well-equipped spa. €€€€

Villa Dubrovnik
Vlaha Bukovca 6; www.villa-dubrovnik.hr
The setting is incomparable in this cliff-top hotel with an indoor/outdoor pool and a beach. The rooftop bar of this stylish member of the Leading Hotels of the World has some of the city's best views. €€€€

Villa Odak
Frana Supila 16; www.villaodak.cro-hr
One of the best budget options in Ploče has functionally furnished rooms with kitchenettes and a shared terrace with great views of the Old Town. It's also handy for beaches, as it's between Banje and Sveti Jakov beaches. €€

Villa Orsula
Frana Supila 14; www.adriaticluxuryhotels.com
Thirteen luxurious rooms are behind the 1939 stone façade of this attractive stone-built boutique hotel. Lush gardens cascade down to the sea and the hotel's beach. Many of the contemporary rooms have sea views and private balconies. €€€€

Pile

Heritage Hotel Nobile
Ulica Između Vrta 6; www.hotel-marcopolo.com
Just beyond the Pile Gate is this peaceful eighteenth-century villa set in the midst of lush gardens – a splendid place for lazy breakfasts. Its six sumptuous suites all have musical or artistic connotations, and two of the ground-floor suites have their own terraces. €€€–€€€€

Hilton Imperial
Marijana Blažića 2; www.hilton.com
Two nineteenth-century buildings make up this grand hotel fronting on

Cliff-top Villa Dubrovnik

to Branitelja Dubrovnika, the road leading uphill from the Pile Gate. Wood and marble finishes give a luxurious air, and many of the rooms have sea views and balconies. There's a large terrace, restaurant, piano bar, indoor pool and gym. €€€–€€€€

Hotel Bellevue
Pera Čingrije 7; www.adriaticluxuryhotels.com
Carved into a cliff is this luxurious hotel built overlooking Miramare Bay. Each of the 93 rooms has a sea view. Lots of local wood and stone have been used in the design, and rooms feature paintings by prestigious Croatian artists. €€€€

Hotel Lero
Iva Vojnovića 14; www.hotel-lero.hr
On the main road between Pile and Lapad, the Lero is a rather dull block of a hotel, but it has a good location, approximately 200 metres/yds from the beach and modern rooms. There's also an outdoor pool and a wellness centre. €€€

Rixos Premium Dubrovnik
Liechtensteinov put 3; allinclusive-collection.com
This sprawling Seventies hotel hugs the cliff overlooking the bay between Lapad and the old town. Contemporary rooms come with balconies, and the restaurants offer Turkish, Croatian and Italian cuisine. It's also home to Dubrovnik's only casino, and the views from the pool are magnificent. Its excellent spa has an area for children. €€€–€€€€

Gruž
Bokun Guesthouse
Obala Stjepana Radića 7; www.bokun-guesthouse.com
Set in a walled garden in a 400-year-old stone farmhouse near the ferry, Bokun Guesthouse features an outdoor pool as well as eight rooms and three apartments. €€

Lapad
Boutique and Beach Hotel Villa Wolff
Šetalište Nika i Meda Pučića 1; http://villa-wolff.hr
A 10-minute drive from the old town leads to this romantic hotel with stunning views across the bay and the pleasant palm tree-shaded terrace of Restaurant Casa. There's no pool, but there's safe swimming from the rocks immediately below. €€€

Hotel Dubrovnik Palace
Masarykov put 20; www.adriaticluxuryhotels.com
Set into the cliff below pine woods, the Hotel Dubrovnik Palace dominates the Lapad headland. All of the 307 rooms have sea views and balconies and the ground-floor bar (one of several) has a wall of glass directly over the sea. There are four pools, a large spa, a secluded beach and a diving centre. €€€€

Hotel Kazbek
Lapadska Obala 25; www.kazbekdubrovnik.com
This five-star boutique hotel is set in a handsome sixteenth-century stone house

Room with a view

Jacuzzi on the terrace, Villa Dubrovnik

on the Lapad side of Gruž harbour. Attractive traditional furnishings are in keeping with the historic setting, enhanced by a heated pool in the large courtyard garden. €€€€

Hotel Komodor
Masarykov put 3E; www.hotelsdubrovnik.com
This is the first in the row of five hotels in this street along the side of Lapad Bay, all of which are part of the Maestral chain. It is the oldest of the five and could do with an update, but it has a restaurant and outdoor pool. €€–€€€

Hotel Kompas
Kardinala Stepinca 21; www.adriaticluxuryhotels.com
This sleek four-star hotel is in a handy spot in front of Lapad Bay. It's smart and modern, with indoor and outdoor pools, a spa, several bars (including the stylish top-floor Zenith Bar) and a restaurant. €€€–€€€€

Hotel Lapad
Lapadska Obala 37; www.hotel-lapad.hr
This attractive nineteenth-century building with a modern wing is on the Lapad side of Gruž harbour, 3km (1.8 miles) from the Pile Gate and on a bus route. Rooms in the new wing have air conditioning. There's a pool and a boat service to the nearest beach in summer. €€€

Hotel More
Kardinala Stepinca 33; www.hotel-more.hr
In a prime position overlooking Lapad Bay is this classy and understated five-star hotel. Try to get a room with a balcony and sea view, but all come with whirlpool baths. The funky Cave Bar, with its dramatic cave-like interior, has become a popular hangout for guests and locals alike, as has its large seafront terrace. €€€€

Hotel Splendid
Masarykov put 6; www.hotelsdubrovnik.com
Another in the Maestral chain, the Splendid backs straight on to the beach and bay. It's somewhat impersonal but comfortable and efficient, and many rooms have balconies and sea views. €€–€€€

Hotel Uvala
Masarykov put 5; www.hotelsdubrovnik.com
Although its exterior is quite plain, the Uvala is the smartest of the five Maestral Lapad hotels. Sea view rooms have minimalist decor, and there's a well-designed wellness centre with indoor and outdoor pools. €€€

Hotel Vis
Masarykov put 2; www.hotelsdubrovnik.com
The rooms are functional but the hotel's location, restaurant terrace and beach make up for the simply furnished interiors. It's worth upgrading to a sea view with a balcony. €€–€€€

Vila Mičika
Mata Vodopića 10; www.vilamicika.hr

Sunsets in Cavtat

Rooms are very basic but it's a good choice for those on a budget who want to be near Lapad's beaches. At least the rooms have their own bathrooms, and for the price it's hard to quibble when you get the use of a kitchenette and a garden with a barbecue. €

Babin Kuk

President Hotel, Valamar Collection
Iva Dulčića 142; www.valamar.com
This large hotel commands the headland, facing out to sea like a great ship. All rooms have balconies and sea views, and there are tennis courts and a gym among its amenities. External lifts take guests down to the hotel's rocky beaches. The other hotels in the Valamar complex include Sunny Dubrovnik by Valamar and Valamar Lacroma Hotel; see website for details. €€€€

Royal Hotels & Resort
Kardinala Stepinca 31; www.royaldubrovnik.com
The other major player on the Babin Kuk peninsula, this group includes the five-star Royal Princess, Neptun, Ariston and Palm. The high-rise Neptun has superb sea views and a restaurant/café terrace that offers one of the best places in Dubrovnik to watch the sun go down (see website for details). €€€–€€€€

Valamar Argosy Hotel
Iva Dulčića 140; www.valamar.com

Suite-to-sea stays in Lopud

Hotel Kompas

This modern four-star hotel is nestled among large landscaped gardens with an infinity pool. Many of the contemporary rooms have sea-facing balconies, and the wellness centre includes a fresh-water indoor swimming pool. Cava Beach is located around 200 metres/yds from the hotel. €€€

Valamar Tirena Hotel
Iva Dulčića 36; www.valamar.com
Airy rooms and plenty of family-friendly facilities make up this refurbished four-star hotel close to Cava Beach. The decor is smart and breezy, and most of the rooms have private balconies. There's an outdoor pool with a swim-up bar, plus water slides and a splash pool for children. €€€

RMH Lopud Lafodia

Orašac

Sun Gardens Dubrovnik
Na Moru 1; www.dubrovniksungardens.com
It's unabashed luxury at this contemporary, cliff-hugging resort 11km (7 miles) west of Dubrovnik, with an enormous spa, infinity pool and its own marina. During the season, a boat shuttles guests to the old town. €€€€

Cavtat

Castelleto
Jurja Dalmatinca 9; www.dubrovnikexperience.com
Friendly 13-room B&B just uphill from the port. Some rooms have balconies with views towards Dubrovnik. There's a nice garden and terrace, and a small outdoor pool, plus an outdoor hot tub. The restaurant serves tapas and local specialities cooked on the grill. €€–€€€

Hotel Croatia
Frankopanska 10; www.adriaticluxuryhotels.com
On a peninsula to the south of the village is this big, modern five-star hotel that's popular with tour agencies. There's sailing, a large pool, children's activities and great views, but it's a bit of a hike down to the beach. €€€–€€€€

Hotel Supetar
Ante Starčevića 27; www.adriaticluxuryhotels.com
Set in two 1920s traditional stone buildings right by the bay, this stylish boutique has a fine-dining restaurant, a wine bar, an outdoor bar and breakfast terrace with wonderful views. €€€€

Remisens Hotel Albatros
Od Žala 1; www.remisens.com
This sprawling modern hotel is a family-friendly place right by the beach. Understated rooms have modern decor and come with balconies, and there are two outdoor pools, one indoor pool and six tennis courts. €€€

Villa Pattiera
Trumbićev put 9; www.villa-pattiera.hr
The birthplace of the Croatian tenor Tino, Pattiera is a cosy four-star by the harbour. Most of the 12 rooms have either a shared or private terrace or balcony, and the hotel also runs the Dalmacija restaurant across the road. €€€

Koločep

TUI BLUE Kalamota Island Resort
Donje Čelo 45; www.tuibluekalamota.com
What was once the Hotel Villas Koločep is now an adults-only all-inclusive resort overlooking Donje Čelo Bay. Modern rooms come with balconies or terraces, and there's a pool if you want a change from the beach in front of the resort. €€–€€€

Šipan

Hotel Božica
Suđurađ 3; www.hotel-bozica.hr
This intimate four-star is only about 15 metres/yds from the sea and comes

Majestic Korčula

with its own beach and mooring for yachts. You'll want one of its sea-facing rooms with a balcony to enjoy splendid views. There's also an outdoor pool and a particularly good restaurant. €€€

Lopud
Hotel Glavović
Obala Iva Kuljevana bb; www.hotel-glavovic.hr
The rooms have simple furnishings, but this friendly family-run hotel is in a great location right on the harbourside. It has a good restaurant, and the beach is practically at your feet. €–€€

RMH Lopud Lafodia
Obala Iva Kuljevana 51; www.lafodiahotel.com
This ultra-modern hotel near the harbour rises up like twin cruise ships divided by cascading café terraces and gardens and topped with a spa. Contemporary rooms are sleek and enhanced by balconies with wonderful sea views and a beach. €€€

Mljet
Hotel Odisej
Pomena; www.adriaticluxuryhotels.com
Parkland surrounds this large hotel overlooking Pomena bay in the Mljet National Park. The decor is in great need of updating, but the hotel is in an enviable position by a beach and has a buzzing beach bar. €€–€€€

PineTree Boutique Apartments
Saplunara 17; www.pinetreemljet.com
Twelve immensely stylish apartments are set in a large stone building in front of Saplunara Bay, all with balconies or terraces with heavenly views of the sea. Interiors are modern and smart, with artwork created by the friendly owner. The family also runs an excellent restaurant, Kod Ante, on the ground floor. €€€

Korčula
Aminess Korčula Heritage Hotel
Obala Franje Tuđmana 5; www.aminess.com
This elegant four-star hotel, right by Korčula Town's harbour, has 20 rooms, a lovely vine-shaded terrace, a good restaurant and wood-panelled public areas. Dating from 1912, it was Korčula's first hotel, and comes with wonderful views of the Pelješac peninsula. €€€

Lešić Dimitri Palace
Don Pavla Poše 1–6; www.ldpalace.com
Set in an eighteenth-century bishop's palace in the heart of the old town is this chic boutique hotel and Relais & Châteaux member. Its opulent rooms hark back to the days of the Silk Road, with suitably Eastern touches. €€€€

Mali Ston
Hotel Vila Koruna
Pelješki put 1; 020-754 999
Famous as Mali Ston's oldest restaurant and purveyor of local oysters, the Vila Koruna has comfortable, functional rooms and a pleasant indoor restaurant as well as a large glass terrace overlooking the bay. €–€€

Restaurants

Eating out in Dubrovnik is a delight, especially during the summer, when nearly all restaurants have outside tables, either on a terrace, a pavement, or right beside the sea. It does help, however, if you like seafood. Meat does feature but fishy things predominate – as you would expect in a city on the shores of the Adriatic. Anyone familiar with Italian food will notice many similarities. You will also see a degree of similarity in Dubrovnik's restaurant menus: from the economical to the expensive, they all feature similar dishes, although the standard of cooking and presentation varies a great deal. Menus are invariably translated into English, and often into German and French as well.

While some establishments are called restaurants, others are known as a *konoba*. A *konoba* was originally a kind of taverna, a somewhat humble or rustic place to eat, and in the rural regions this is still the case, but in the city the two words are interchangeable. You may find a relatively expensive restaurant calling itself a *konoba*, while a more basic one is known as a restaurant.

Local people usually eat lunch around 1.30pm and dinner at about 9pm, but restaurateurs are so used to catering to foreign visitors, who provide most of their trade, that they will serve lunch from midday throughout most of the afternoon, and dinner from round 6pm. At the height of the season, many restaurants carry on serving dinner until about 11pm. Many close in winter.

Some restaurants impose a cover charge (couvert) per person, typically about €2–€4 each. This should be made clear on the menu before you order. If you want tap water rather than bottled water, ask for "*obična* (obeechna) *voda*", although some waiters will insist on giving you still bottled water. Ordering fish by the kilo can be an expensive business, so make certain you and the waiter know how much you've ordered and what the price will be.

As in many tourist hot spots, Dubrovnik has its share of restaurants whose staff tout for business in Stradun during meal

> ### Price categories
> Approximate prices are based on a two-course meal for one, with a glass of house wine:
> € = under €30
> €€ = €30–50
> €€€ = over €50

Above 5 Rooftop Restaurant lives up to its name

times. As the city also has its share of mediocre restaurants, don't feel compelled to pay attention to the touts. They'll soon get bored and move on to someone else.

Old Town

360°
Svetog Dominika; www.360dubrovnik.com
A medieval arsenal set in the City Walls is the setting for this sophisticated Michelin-starred restaurant with fantastic views of the Old Port. They don't skimp on top-class ingredients here: turbot, venison, lobster and the ubiquitous truffle feature on a Mediterranean menu. It's a magnet in the season, so book ahead. Closed in winter and Mondays. Dinner only. €€€

Long-running restaurant Kamenice

Above 5 Rooftop Restaurant
Od Sigurate 4; www.hotelstarigrad.com
Once you've climbed up about five flights of stairs, you're rewarded with one of the most romantic views of Dubrovnik's old town. The rooftop restaurant at Hotel Stari Grad is tiny and it's worth reserving a table for beautifully cooked Mediterranean cuisine. Closed in winter. €€€

Azur
Pobijana 10; www.azurvision.com
Croatia meets Asia in this laid-back little restaurant tucked away near the city walls not far from the Aquarium. The innovative menu is heavy on curry, Japanese and Thai spices livening up chicken, beef and fish dishes in relaxed surroundings. Closed in winter. €€

Barba
Boškovićeva 5; 091-205 3488
Between Prijeko and Stradun is this unpretentious little seafood café with a casually rustic interior – just the spot for a quick but delicious lunch. Try the octopus burger or tempura prawns. €

Bota Šare Oyster Bar & Sushi Bar
Od Pustijerne bb; 020-324 034; www.bota-sare.hr
Oysters from Ston are given the Japanese treatment in this sleek modern restaurant by the Cathedral. In fact, most of the Adriatic fruits of the sea

Lamb dish at Above 5 Rooftop Restaurant

are beautifully turned into sushi, teriyaki and tempura delights. €€

Bura Bistro and Bar
Bunićeva Poljana; www.burabistro-dubrovnik.com

In one of Dubrovnik's buzziest squares, wedged between the Cathedral and the Old Town market, Bura Bistro combines creative cocktails with fresh seafood dishes, pizzas and plenty of Mediterranean flavours. Live jazz adds to the lively atmosphere. €€

Dalmatino
Prijeko ulica 15; www.dalmatino-dubrovnik.com

This cosy restaurant moved to bigger premises in Prijeko, offering more space to enjoy its fresh seafood and meat dishes which include black ink risotto, lobster and a daily catch. €€–€€€

Kamenice
Gundulićeva Poljana 8; 020-323 682

Tables spread out in front of this long-established restaurant where fish figures prominently on the menu. The grilled squid is particularly good, and they also specialise in oysters, after which the restaurant is named. €–€€

Konoba Aquarius
Ulica Kneza Damjana Jude 4; 091-526 8790

Just a few steps away from the Aquarium is this laid-back *konoba* with simply grilled fish and meat dishes. The secluded garden is an unexpected treat. Closed in winter. €–€€

Lady Pi-Pi
Antuninska 23; 020-321 154

Don't let the name put you off this appealing place in the shadow of the city walls north of Prijeko. Meat dishes are cooked in front of you on the open barbecue under the vine-covered terrace, and a higher terrace gives you great views of the old town. You can't book ahead, so be prepared to queue. €–€€

Lucin Kantun
Od Sigurate 4a; 020-321 003

Just off Stradun is this pleasant, unpretentious little place with friendly staff and an open kitchen. The restaurant makes good use of locally grown vegetables and serves some excellent tapas dishes. €€

Mea Culpa
Za Rokom 3; www.meaculpa-pizzeria.com

Some of the biggest pizzas in town are served at wooden benches in a narrow street parallel to Stradun. Don't be afraid to ask for one to share – they are large enough. Resist the pleading eyes of the resident cats if you are strong-minded enough. Closed in winter. €€

Nishta
Prijeko bb; 020-322 088

True vegan food is hard to come by in Croatia, so it's not surprising that this small restaurant on the corner of Prijeko and Palmotičeva has a devoted following. Asian, Middle Eastern and Mexican flavours mingle with local dishes, and there are gluten-free options. €

Pavement tables at Proto

Pizzeria Oliva
Lučarica 5; www.pizzeriaolivadubrovnik.com
In a narrow lane behind St Blaise Church is this lively pizzeria, where they serve a large selection of good-value pizzas along with more basic pasta dishes and salads. €

Proto
Široka 1; www.esculaprestaurants.com
Established in 1886 and still going strong, Proto, just off Stradun at the Pile Gate end, serves very good meat and fish at pavement tables, indoors or (most popular) on an upstairs terrace. Recommended by the Michelin guide, so book ahead in high season. Closed in winter. €€€

Restaurant Dubrovnik
Marojice Kaboge 5; www.restaurantdubrovnik.com
One of the stalwarts of Dubrovnik's fine-dining scene is a welcoming and relaxed place to try some beautifully presented dishes. Choose between two tasting menus and à la carte, all of which champion local ingredients creatively. €€€

Restaurant Magdalena
Pucić Palace Hotel; Od Puča 1; www.thepucicpalace.com
This roof-terrace restaurant is smart without being stuffy and has lovely views over the old town. Some dishes have a Middle Eastern flavour, and there is also plenty of fish. €€€

Rozario
Prijeko 1; www.konoba-rozario.hr
One of the best of the Prijeko restaurants is close to the Dominican monastery and serves excellent Dalmatian food in a cosy dining room or at a few tables in a shady corner outside. As it's not very big, it's a good idea to book. Closed in winter. €€

Spaghetteria Toni
Božidarevićeva 14; www.spaghetteria-toni.com
Just off Puča, this is the place for large helpings of very well-cooked homemade pasta, risottos and pizzas. Closed in winter. €€

Stara Loza
Prijeko 22; www.prijekopalace.com
The restaurant on the ground floor of the Prijeko Palace is as classy as the hotel itself. They do an imaginative take on local cuisine and add a few international dishes. There's also a dining salon on the third floor, and if you want to dine on the rooftop restaurant terrace, you'll have to book ahead. €€

Taj Mahal
Nikole Gučetića 2; www.tajmahal-dubrovnik.com
Get a taste of neighbouring Bosnia in this cave-like restaurant decorated in Ottoman style. Dishes include Bosnian staples such as *ćevapčići*, spicy meat rissoles and savoury pastries known as *burek*, filled with meat or cheese. There's another branch in Hotel Lero. €€

Proto's popular upstairs terrace

Presentation is key at Proto

Bistro Tavulin
Cvijete Zuzorić; www.bistrotavulin.com
Choose between the cosy stone-walled interior or one of the outside tables squeezed into the marble lane opposite the Rector's Palace. Bistro Tavulin offers well-presented dishes that span the Mediterranean but feature local ingredients. €€

Ploče
Bistro Revelin
Sv. Dominika bb; 099-205 6220
The Revelin is better known for its cavernous disco inside this medieval fort overlooking the Old Port. But its outdoor restaurant under giant trees comes with glorious views and decent Italian-influenced meat and seafood dishes. Closed in winter. €€–€€€

Ezza Steak & Cocktail Bar
Hvarska ulica2; https://ezzarestaurant.com
Enjoy fabulous views of the city walls, the port and the sea just beyond on Ezza's pleasant terrace. Co-founded by top Bosnian footballer Edin Džeko, Ezza focuses on steak, burgers and other meat dishes as well as seafood. But you'll also find some vegetarian options. €€€

Gusta Me
Hvarska 2; www.gustame-dubrovnik.com
You get lovely views of the old port in this buzzing restaurant just outside the Ploče Gate. Good-value meat and seafood dishes are served on a large sheltered terrace, and it's worth booking ahead during high season. Closed in winter. €€

Konoba Kenova
Put od Bosanke 8; www.kenova.hr
Take in marvellous views of the old port from one of the tables on the stepped pavement while you enjoy Dalmatian classics as well as innovative dishes. Try the filo roll of octopus with polenta, or slow-cooked lamb shank. Closed in winter. €€

Pile
Dubravka 1836 Restaurant & Café
Brsalje 1; www.nautikarestaurants.com/dubravka-restaurant-cafe
Just outside the Pile Gate and overlooking Fort Lovrijenac, Dubravka's large terrace gives diners magnificent views. The varied menu offers generous pizzas and pastas as well as salads, fresh fish and meat dishes. The cocktails are worth checking out. Closed in winter. €€–€€€

Nautika
Brsalje 3; www.nautikarestaurants.com
This Dubrovnik institution had been hosting the great and the good for decades, serving top-class seafood by the water's edge just outside the Pile Gate. Its beautiful setting offers amazing views over Lovrijenac and Bokar forts. Closed in winter. €€€

Posat
Uz Posat 1 (just outside Pile Gate); www.posat-dubrovnik.com

Harbourfront restaurants

The setting, fronting a car park, is unprepossessing, but once you are settled on the upper terrace your view is over Fort Lovrijenac. It's upscale dining with a focus on Mediterranean seafood. Closed in winter. €€€

Sesame
Dante Alighieria 2; www.sesame.hr
This pleasant little restaurant serving good risottos and homemade pasta dishes is in a narrow street off the main Ante Starčevića road leading west from Pile Gate. It's popular with students, as one of the university faculties is nearby. It also has simple rooms for rent. Closed in winter. €€

Mount Srđ
Panorama
Upper Cable Car Station, Mount Srđ; www.nautikarestaurants.com
The views are incomparable in this restaurant at the top of the cable car station. And the food, if a little pricey, is worthy of the trip up to Mount Srđ either via cable car or the 1-hour hike. It's a good stop for lunch or to catch the sunset. Closed in winter. €€–€€€

Gruž
Dubrovnik Beer Company
Obala Ivana Pavla II 15; www.dubrovackapivovara.hr
If you like craft beer and hefty burgers, join the lively crowd at what has become a Gruž institution. There are tables inside and outside the brewery, which is also a venue for live music. Closed in winter. €

The view from Panorama

Konoba-Pizzeria Blidinje
Lapadska Obala 21; http://konoba-blidinje.com
On the Lapad side of Gruž's harbour is a good-value pizzeria that also does slow-cooked meat dishes *ispod peke* – under an iron bell. These should be ordered a couple of hours in advance. Try to get a table on the upstairs terrace with views of the harbour. €€

Porat Restaurant
Obala Stjepana Radića 30; www.porat-restaurant-bar-eatbu.hr
Dalmatian seafood and meat dishes get equal billing in this friendly restaurant between Gruž's market and ferry port. There's also a fine selection of pasta and risotto dishes along with generous-sized salads. Closed in winter. €€

Michelin-starred 360°

Bougenvila in Cavtat

Restaurant Orsan
Ivana Zajca 2;
www.restaurant-orsan-dubrovnik.com
Slightly further up the waterside on the Lapad side of Gruž's harbour, Orsan (the name means boathouse) serves good-quality fish, meat and rice dishes. It's right on the jetty in a lively setting, with views of all the action on the harbour. €€

Urban & Veggie Vegan Restaurant
Obala Stjepana Radića 13;
www.urbanveggie.restaurant
Another rare sighting of a vegan restaurant in Croatia, this time along the bustling area of Gruž harbour. There are innovative breakfast dishes to go with classic vegan burgers and Asian-inspired noodle and rice dishes. €

Lapad and Babin Kuk

Bacchus Bistro
Ćira Carića; bistrobacchus.com
This unpretentious local restaurant is a relaxed choice for brunch or an informal meal, especially if you're on an e-bike tour, as there's a charging point on site as well as e-bike rentals. Snack on spring rolls and dumplings, or fill up on a burger, grilled fish or a steak. €

Fish & Seafood Restaurant Casa
Šetalište Nika i Meda Pucića 1;
www.restaurant-casa.com
The restaurant at the Villa Wolff is in an enviable setting right on Lapad Bay. The menu changes with the seasons but will always include fresh fish and seafood, and Dalmatian specialities. €€

Levanat
Šetalište Nika i Meda Pucića 15;
www.restaurant-levanat.com
Follow the seaside path from Restaurant Casa and you will come to this delightful place. Prawns in honey with sage is among the more unusual dishes, but standards such as stuffed squid and mussels in a *buzara* sauce (white wine and garlic) are excellent, too. Or you can just have a drink and watch the sun set over the sea. €€–€€€

Restaurant Komin
Iva Dulčića 136; www.restaurant-komin.com
Unless you are staying in one of the Babin Kuk hotels, you are unlikely to stumble across this place, but it's close to the terminus of the No. 6 bus. Set in a family-oriented little park with a large terrace, it specialises in grilled meat and fish, including meat cooked *ispod peke*. Closed in winter. €–€€

Restaurant Pantarul
Kralja Tomislava 1; www.pantarul.com
The focus is on local seasonal ingredients in this friendly restaurant with contemporary interiors. Well-crafted dishes include slowly braised ox cheeks as well as expertly grilled Dalmatian fish. €–€€

Restaurant Zoë
Šetalište Nike i Media Pucića 17b;
www.royaldubrovnik.com

Local wines

Stupendous views of the bay go a long way to make up for a somewhat limited menu. Fresh seafood is the star, of course, especially a whole fish baked in salt. But there are also meat and veggie options. Closed in winter. €€–€€€

Shizuku Japanese Cuisine
Kneza Domagoja 1; 020-311 493

If you're in the mood for a change from Croatian cuisine, then try these plates of sushi, tempura and classic Japanese and Thai dishes. It gets very busy in the summer, so it's best to book ahead – especially if you want a table outside on the terrace. Closed in winter. €–€€

Lopud
Konoba Mandrač
Obala Iva Kuljevana 49;
www.restaurantmandrac.com

Enjoy the sea views from Mandrač's waterside location as you choose between Asian-inspired dishes and classic Dalmatian seafood and grilled meats. €€

Konoba Peggy
Narikla 22; www.pavlovic-pension-lopud.com

Just a few metres from the harbour, this is a popular spot with a large leafy terrace and substantial helpings of fish and seafood. It can get busy, as day-trippers are often pointed in this direction and may arrive in a bunch. €–€€

Restaurant Obala
Obala Iva Kuljevana 18; www.obalalopud.com

The view at Restaurant Zoë

There are tables so close to the water you could almost dip your toes in as you eat. There is also a covered terrace and an indoor dining area. Fish couldn't be fresher and the salads are great too, especially when washed down with local wine. Closed in winter. €€–€€€

Koločep
Villa Ruža
Donje Čelo; 020-757 020

The setting is sublime in this 1930s stone villa in a pine-shaded garden at the far end of the seaside promenade. If you can take your eyes off the sea views, tuck into seafood risottos or whatever the fishermen have brought in that day. Closed in winter. €€

Šipan
BOWA
Pakljena 3; www.bowa-dubrovnik.com

BOWA stands for "best of what's around", and it's almost too prosaic a name for this dreamy restaurant tucked into a cove near Suđurađ and best reached by boat. It's pricey but worth it for the incredibly fresh fish cooked superbly well. The setting is wonderful: many tables are under bamboo-roofed cabanas, and you won't be able to resist a post-prandial swim in the cove right in front of the restaurant. Closed in winter. €€€

Cavtat
Bougenvila
Obala Ante Starčevića 9; www.bugenvila.online

A simple dish of anchovies

Classic Dalmatian cooking is given a modern touch in this smart harbourside restaurant with friendly service. Seafood-lovers can indulge in steamed lobster or sea bass tartare, while carnivores can try braised wild boar cheeks. Closed in winter. €€–€€€

Dalmacija
Trumbićev put 9; www.villa-pattiera.hr
Set in a busy little triangle at the southern end of the harbour promenade, the popular Dalmacija has been in business since 1979. As you would expect from the name, it offers Dalmatian cooking, mainly fish but also good meat dishes, and is usually bustling and busy at lunchtime. Closed in winter. €€–€€€

Konoba Ivan
Tiha put 8; www.konoba-ivan.eatbu.com
On the other side of the peninsula (but only a few hundred metres if you go across the narrow neck), Konoba Ivan is a small, lively place right by the water's edge where fresh fish and grilled meat, accompanied by carafes of house wine, make a good lunch. Closed in winter. €€

Zino
Obala Ante Starčevića 5; 020-478 300
This cheerful spot by the harbour has a few wok dishes to go with its mainly Dalmatian menu of fish, seafood, meat and pasta. The pizzas are very good value. €–€€

Mljet
Konoba Galija
Pomena 7, Pomena; 099-5478 935
One of a string of little restaurants along Pomena's harbourside (facing the Hotel Odisej across the bay), Galija has tables in a leafy arbour and live lobsters swimming in a huge tank. Portions are generous, so feel free to share. €€

Konoba Herc
Pomena bb; 020-744 151
The furthest of the restaurants lining Pomena's harbour is a laid-back spot with wonderful views of the water, especially at sunset. Try the salt-baked fish or octopus cooked slowly under a *peka*. €€

Restoran Stermasi
Saplunara; www.stermasi.hr
Set on a hillside overlooking the rocky bay is this friendly restaurant that specialises in dishes cooked *ispod peke* – under a cast-iron bell. Allow a couple of hours if you order one – or order it in advance – as it's the epitome of slow cooking. There's even a vegetarian option, which is a rarity here. €€–€€€

Stella Maris
Polače 22, Polače; www.stellamaris-croatia.com
Another Polače restaurant with a harbourfront site, this one is so close to the ferry dock that you could sit here until the gangplank is about to go up. It offers the usual seafood and grilled meat dishes – plus meat and

Cavtat's waterfront is lined with restaurants

fish cooked *ispod peke* – along with local wine and friendly service. €€

Korčula
7 Seas Restaurant and Bar
Obala Dr Franje Tuđmana bb; www.aminess.com

The restaurant at Hotel Korčula has an elegant dining room and a pretty vine-covered terrace opposite the ferry dock. There's an extensive list of local wines to accompany the excellent fish dishes. €€–€€€

Konoba Feral
Lumbarda 63; 020-712 090

This friendly place on one of the little coves in the fishing village of Lumbarda south of Korčula Town offers wonderful views of the beach to go with plentiful seafood. Grab a table on the main terrace or on the little over-the-water terrace and feast on Dalmatian seafood. Closed in winter. €€

LD Restaurant
Don Pavla Poše 1-6; www.ldrestaurant.com

Michelin-starred dining by the water's edge in the most relaxed surroundings makes LD Restaurant a must-visit if you enjoy exquisitely presented but unstuffy food. The kitchen has its own organic garden to go with local Dalmatian ingredients, which come in both a tasting menu (with a vegetarian option) or à la carte. Closed in winter. €€€

Restaurant Filippi
Šetalište Petra Kanavelića;
www.restaurantfilippi.com

Featuring beautiful sea views, this fine restaurant serves excellent seafood and home-made pasta dishes. Leave space for the delicious desserts, and the wine selection doesn't disappoint either. Closed in winter. €€€

Mali Ston
All the restaurants in Mali Ston specialise in the oysters and mussels that are cultivated here, and of which they are very proud. They are the reason people flock here for Sunday lunch, but the venues also serve a range of other seafood and fish, and some meat dishes.

Bota Šare Restaurant & Oyster Bar
Mali Ston bb; www.bota-sare.hr

The island's renowned oysters figure prominently – not surprisingly – in this cavernous, stone-walled dining room with lots of outside tables on a waterside terrace. There is also a very good selection of seafood risotto, shellfish and pasta dishes as well as steaks. €€

Villa Koruna
Mali Ston bb; www.vila-koruna.hr

The best known of the Mali Ston restaurants, the Koruna has a vast, glass-covered terrace, a cosy, old-fashioned dining room, and fish swimming in large tanks (as well as two large turtles, which are not for clients' consumption). Presentation is great and the food is good, too. €€

Nightlife

Dubrovnik's nightlife tends to be concentrated on its many cafés and bars, rather than the sort of large beach clubs you find in other Croatian resorts. While there are a few nightclubs outside the edges of the Old Town, most people gather on the outdoor terraces of bars that fill the streets and squares.

On warm summer evenings, you'll see people spilling outside on to the steps of the narrow streets that lead to Prijeko off Stradun, as the tiny bars within will be packed out within minutes.

The following listings are just a selection of the highlights of Dubrovnik's nightlife. For an overview of entertainment in the city, see page 22. Many of the bars and clubs are seasonal, with a fair number closing from early October and not reopening until Easter.

Concert venues

Lazareti
Frana Supila 8; 095-791 5033

The seventeenth-century quarantine barracks just outside the City Walls is Dubrovnik's leading cultural and arts venue. It stages everything from folklore performances by Lindo Folklore Ensemble to underground club nights, mini festivals and outdoor film screenings. The complex also contains a huddle of independent art galleries and artisanal workshops.

Bars

La Bodega
Stradun; 994 851 301

This smart bar is a lively and popular meeting point in the Stradun, where people snack on sushi, sashimi and burgers over drinks.

Buzz Bar
Prijeko 21; www.thebuzzbar.wixsite.com/buzz

Situated among Prijeko's sea of touristy restaurants is this chilled-out bar with a bright modern interior and occasional live guitar sets.

Love Bar
Andrije Hebranga; www.lovebardubrovnik.com

Head out towards Gruž harbour for rooftop cocktails and some of the best views of Dubrovnik, especially at dusk when the sun goes down in a fiery blaze.

Mr Goodlife Gin Pub & Pizza
Ulica uz Tabor; 097-748 4657

Order a cocktail and pizza and listen to live music on the small terrace of this friendly bar outside the Ploče Gate, where the occasional bout of dancing is known to break out.

Troubadour Jazz Brasserie
Bunićeva Poljana 2; 091-977 3983

Stradun, the epicentre of Dubrovnik's nightlife

This Dubrovnik institution has a large terrace in the shadow of the Cathedral, where live jazz (and music vaguely resembling jazz) is played on weekends.

D'Vino
Palmitoćeva 4a; www.dvino.net

It's a tight squeeze in this busy wine bar off Stradun near the Pile Gate, where people are wedged into the narrow street enjoying excellent Croatian wines when they're not ensconced in the cosy vaulted interior.

Wine Bar Škar
Dropčeva 2; www.lekri.eu

Choose from two branches of Škar Winery's wine bars – one in the Old Town just off Stradun, and the other on the Lapad side of Gruž harbour at Lapadska Obala 17.

Clubs
Banje Beach Nightclub
Frana Supila 10/B; www.banjebeach.com

The daytime atmosphere of this bar on Banje Beach becomes more sophisticated as the sun goes down and everyone grabs a cocktail. In the height of summer, it's open till 6am. Closed in winter.

Culture Club Revelin
Ulica Svetog Dominika 3; www.clubrevelin.com

The imposing fortress hosts club nights with international DJs as well as live bands. Clubbers can take a breather on the giant terrace with great views of the Old Town. Closed in January.

Elyx Night Club
Brsalje ulica 8; https://dubrovniknightlife.com

This lively nightclub just outside the Pile Gate plays an eclectic mix of music in a friendly atmosphere. Open Friday to Sunday only, with 6am closings on Saturday and Sunday.

Casinos
Merit Casino Libertas
Liechtensteinov put 3; www.meritcasinos.com

Dubrovnik's only casino is in the glittering setting of the five-star Rixos Premium Dubrovnik.

Theatre
Marin Držić Theatre
Pred Dvorom 3; www.kmd.hr

This neo-Renaissance theatre dating from 1865 is home to a repertory theatre company that stages Croatian and international productions. It's one of the main venues during the Summer Festival.

Cinema
Kinematografi Dubrovnik
Luža; www.kinematografi.org

Dubrovnik's only year-round cinema is located right by the clock tower in Luža Square. Croatian films are screened here as well as big-hitting Hollywood blockbusters, the latter usually with subtitles.

Essentials

Accessible travel

The smooth marble streets of the old town make it easy for people in wheelchairs to explore the old town. Many hotels have been updated to include facilities for people with disabilities, and there is a wheelchair-accessible public toilet at Pile Gate. People with limited mobility will find it difficult to climb the steps to the higher street and to walk the ramparts. However, there is a transporter that can be booked in advance, and you can also rent wheelchairs (020-418 810).

Age restrictions

The age of consent in Croatia is 15. To drive legally in Croatia you must be at least 18 and have your full licence. Children under 12 are not allowed in the front seat of cars. The legal drinking age is 18.

Budgeting

Dubrovnik is one of Croatia's more expensive destinations. The following is a general guide to how to budget.

A glass of house wine will cost about €7. A main course in a cheap restaurant is about €20, and in a more expensive restaurant will be about €32.

It can be difficult to find budget accommodation in Dubrovnik as more and more luxury hotels spring up. A double room in a cheap hotel will cost about €75 out of season; a moderate hotel in high season is about €200, and the luxury hotels will be well in excess of €350.

Buses are reasonably cheap, with fares at around €2.50 if bought on the bus and €1.73 if bought at a kiosk. Ferry tickets vary enormously, but usually start at €3 for short trips, e.g. to Šipan. A taxi from the airport will cost about €35–€40.

The major museums and sites charge from €5 to €40, with discounts for students and children, and some prices are seasonal. Admission to churches is free.

If you plan to pack in a lot of sights and explore the area, then a Dubrovnik Card (www.dubrovnikcard.com) could be good value. Available for one, three and seven days, it gives you free public transport as well as free entry into the top attractions including the city walls and the Rector's Palace. It's about 10 percent cheaper if you buy it online, and you also receive discounts in participating shops and restaurants.

Children

Most hotels, restaurants and cafés are very accommodating to families. In many places children under three can stay free, and discounts are often available for accommodation, travel and food for under-12s and even

Dubrovnik's baroque cathedral

older teenagers. Beaches offer plenty of water-based activities for children as well as dry sporting facilities for older children. There are a few sandy beaches on some of the islands, but Dubrovnik's beaches are pebbly or rocky. If you don't bring swimming shoes, they're easily available in shops.

The areas with the biggest selection of family-friendly hotels are Lapad and Babin Kuk, which is also where the most extensive beach facilities are.

Clothing

Most styles of dressing are tolerated, but Croatians like to dress smartly and you will blend in more easily if you do too. Visitors of both sexes should avoid short shorts and bare shoulders when visiting churches. Topless bathing is not actually forbidden on most beaches but it is not common. There is, however, a naturist beach on the island of Lokrum (signposted FKK). For comfort, wear loose, light clothes in summer, but remember that sudden downpours do happen. A waterproof and umbrella are useful, as is a sweater or jacket for evenings. Flip-flop sandals, sunhats, sarongs and other beach cover-ups are easy to find when you get here.

Crime and safety

Dubrovnik is, on the whole, a safe city, and crime rates are low. As elsewhere, of course, take care of your property, keep an eye on your luggage, and don't flash large sums of money around. If you are a victim of a crime, report it to the police (tel: 192). You will need a police report, made within 24 hours, if you want to make an insurance claim.

Customs

Visitors from EU countries have no limits on what they can import, as long as they can prove it is for personal use. Visitors from outside the EU can bring two litres of table wine, two litres of liqueur or dessert wine, 1 litre of spirits, 200 cigarettes or 100 cigarillos or 50 cigars or 250g of tobacco into Croatia duty free. If you are carrying more than a total of €10,000 in cash or cheques, you must declare it at customs.

Embassies and consulates

The UK no longer has a consulate in Dubrovnik. The nearest one is in Split, at Obala Hrvatskog Narodnog Preporoda 10; 01-6009 100.

Electricity

The standard is 220 volts. Sockets take plugs with two round pins, so UK visitors need adapters. Visitors from the US and Canada need transformers for 110-volt appliances.

Emergency numbers

General emergency number: 112
Ambulance and medical emergency: 194
Fire service: 193
Police: 192
Assistance on the roads: 1987

The tranquil harbour

Search and rescue at sea: 195

Etiquette

Croatians tend to be quite reserved with strangers. When addressing strangers, it is polite to use the honorific *gospodine* (for a man), *gospodo* (for a married woman) or *gospodice* (for a young unmarried woman).

Festivals

2–3 February: Celebrations in honour of Sveti Vlaho (St Blaise).
February–March: Carnival, with colourful processions in Stradun and masked balls in the large hotels. Processions are also held in Cavtat.
Mid-March: The Festival of Oysters, Ston and Mali Ston.
March–April: Good Friday processions. Easter Sunday: processions after Mass and the blessing of the town at the land and sea gates.
Late May: Pelješac Bridge Run, a race across the Pelješac Bridge.
Mid-July–late August: Dubrovnik Summer Festival.
July–August: Cavtat Summer Festival: male voice choirs and water polo tournaments.
29 July: St Theodor's Day in Korčula is celebrated with the Moreška (Sword Dance Festival).
Mid-September: Epidaurus Festival (music, art, drama) in Cavtat.
Late September–early October: Grape harvest festival in Pelješac and Korčula, Ston Wall Marathon in Ston.
Late October: Dubrovnik Film Festival and Dubrovnik Good Food Festival.
Late November–early December: Dubrovnik Winter Festival.

Health

There are no particular health hazards in Croatia, and no vaccinations are required. Dubrovnik's tap water is safe to drink and it tastes fine, but bottled water *(voda)* is widely available if you prefer it. Mosquitoes can be a problem in summer, so take protective cream or lotion and perhaps invest in an appliance that plugs into a socket in your hotel room.

Citizens of Britain, Ireland and most European countries are entitled to free medical care. EU citizens can use their EHIC (European Health Insurance Card), and British citizens should carry their Global Health Insurance Card (GHIC). However, it is advisable to take out a separate travel insurance policy as neither card covers repatriation costs.

Hospitals

Dubrovnik's hospital is in Lapad at Roka Mišetića 2, 020-431 777, and has a 24-hour emergency department (194).

There is also the Poliknika Marini Med, at Ante Starčevića 45, 020-400 500. There is also a dental surgery, Dental Care Dubrovnik, at Ulica Iva Vojnovića 30, 020-333 417.

Hotel receptionists will be able to advise you about medical and dental services for non-urgent matters.

Resting near the Large Fountain of Onofrio

Chemists

There are chemists *(ljekarne)* all over the city. Main ones include: Ljekarna Gruž, Obala Pape Ivana Pavle II 9, 020-418 990. Ljekarna Kod Zvonika, Placa, 020-321 133. Ljekarna Kod Male Braće, Placa 30, 020-321 411. Ljekarna Lapad, Mata Vodopića 30, 020-436 778.

Hours and holidays

Most shops are generally open Mon–Sat 9am–8pm in summer, although some close on Saturday afternoon. In winter, they may close for lunch. Supermarkets stay open till 9pm and also open on Sunday. Most markets operate from around 7am until noon or 1pm. Main post offices are generally open Mon–Fri 8am–7pm, Sat 8am–1pm. Hours for larger banks are typically Mon–Fri 8am–7pm, Sat 8am–noon.

Public holidays

1 January New Year's Day
6 January Epiphany
3 February Sveti Vlaho (St Blaise)
March/April Easter Monday
1 May Labour Day
June Corpus Christi (dates vary)
22 June Anti-Fascist Resistance Day
25 June Statehood Day
5 August Homeland Thanksgiving Day
15 August Feast of the Assumption
8 October Independence Day
1 November All Saints' Day
25–26 December Christmas and St Stephen's Day

Internet facilities

There are some internet cafés in Dubrovnik, but most hotels have WiFi, as do many bars and cafés, so don't hesitate to ask for the code if you're eating or drinking there.

LGBTQ+ travellers

Croatia is a Roman Catholic country, and homosexuality is tolerated but not embraced. The gay scene in Dubrovnik is minimal in spite of the fact that it's a popular destination for LGBTQ+ travellers. Troubadour Jazz Brasserie in the old town is a popular meeting point, as is the nudist beach on the island of Lokrum.

Media

Online English-language newspapers and websites include *The Dubrovnik Times* (www.thedubrovniktimes.com), which covers the city specifically, and *Croatia Week* (www.croatiaweek.com).

Money

Currency

Croatia's currency is the euro, which the country adopted in January 2023.

Changing money

Foreign currency can be exchanged at banks, exchange bureaux, post offices

Lace stall

and most tourist agencies and hotels. Banking hours are generally Monday–Friday 8am–7pm (8am–5pm for smaller branches), Saturday 8am–noon/1pm (weekdays only for smaller branches).

Credit and debit cards

Most hotels, restaurants and larger shops accept credit cards, but it is always wise to check in advance. Cash machines (ATMs) are found throughout the city, especially in Stradun, and in Cavtat and Korčula, but are harder to find on the smaller islands. Stand-alone ATMs (usually yellow) charge a higher rate for foreign withdrawals than ATMs associated with banks.

Taxes

All prices shown are net, i.e. what you actually have to pay. If you look closely you may see that an amount for VAT (PDF) is detailed on some bills, but this does not mean it is extra, as the tax is built into the price.

Tipping

Service charge is rarely added to restaurant bills, so a tip of 10 percent could be added if you are happy with the service. In cheaper restaurants, you can just leave any coins from the change. For taxi drivers, just round up the amount. Hotel porters should be tipped if they are helpful, and cleaning staff should be given an amount commensurate with your length of stay.

Post

The main post offices *(pošta)* are in Široka 8 (off Stradun) and Vukovarska 16. Stamps are sold in post offices and in some shops that sell postcards. It usually takes about two weeks for a postcard to get from Dubrovnik to another European destination, but it can be faster.

Religion

Croatia is an overwhelmingly Roman Catholic country, although there is a small minority of Muslims and Serbian Orthodox residents in Dubrovnik. There is also a tiny Jewish population in the city.

Smoking

There is a smoking ban on all enclosed public places including bars, restaurants and cafés. However, be prepared for plenty of smoke in outdoor terraces of cafés and restaurants – and, occasionally, indoors.

Telephones

The prefix for Croatia is +385. The code for Dubrovnik and Southern Dalmatia is 020. To call Croatia from outside the country, first dial your international access code followed by the code for Croatia. When calling from abroad, omit the initial 0 in the regional access code. Directory enquiries: 11888. General information: 18981. International directory assistance: 11802

Street musicians on Stradun

Public phones can be used only with phone cards, which can be bought in post offices and at newsagents' kiosks. You can make international calls from a phone box but it may be preferable to phone from a post office where you make your call then pay afterwards. Mobile phone numbers begin with 09.

Mobile phones: Roaming charges typically apply to non-EU citizens using their mobile phones in Europe. For UK citizens, free roaming no longer automatically applies, as a result of Brexit. Some providers may still offer free or discounted roaming, but its advisable to check the terms of your contract before travelling.

If data roaming charges do apply, you may be better off purchasing an eSIM as this is generally a more cost-effective solution.

Time zones

Croatia follows Central European Time (GMT+1). From the last Sunday in March to the last Sunday in October, clocks are advanced one hour (GMT+2).

Toilets

There are public toilets in the old town, but they cost about €1. Owners of bars and cafés won't be pleased if you use the facilities without buying a drink, and some need a key or a code. The only free public toilet is on the City Walls.

Tourist information

The main tourist offices are at Brsalje 5, just up from the Pile Gate (020-323 887), which is the most helpful. There is another in Gruž, at Obala Ivana Pavla II 1 (020-417 983), and in Lapad, Masarykov put 3 (020-437 460; open seasonally). Email for information: info@tzdubrovnik.hr.

Tours and guides

There are a number of tour agencies that organise trips to the Elaphite Islands, to Korčula, Ston and the Pelješac peninsula, to the Neretva River delta, to Mljet, and further afield to Montenegro, Mostar, Sarajevo and other destinations.

Elite Travel (Vukovarska 17; 020-358 200; www.elite.hr) runs tours as well as day cruises on the lovely galleon *Tirena*. Amico Tours (Čubranovićeva 11a; 91 444 4445; www.amico-tours.com) has an interesting programme of full-day, half-day and boat tours. Adriana Cavtat (098-485 949; www.adriana-cavtat.com) does Elaphite Islands trips and others along the Dubrovnik Riviera (Lokrum, Mlini, Plat), many on attractive old-style sailing boats. Adriatic Explore (020-323 400; www.adriatic-explore.com) also does day trips, private tours and boat rental.

Transport

Arrival by air

From the UK, flights take about 2 hours 40 minutes. In summer there

Sponza Palace

are frequent direct flights with British Airways (www.ba.com), Croatia Airlines (www.croatiaairlines.com), easyJet (www.easyjet.com), Jet2 (www.jet2.com) and Ryanair (www.ryanair.com). There are a number of charter flights from holiday companies including TUI (020-3451 2688; www.tui.co.uk).

Currently, United Airlines operates a direct flight from Newark to Dubrovnik, but US direct flights to Dubrovnik seem to come and go in regularity. There are no direct flights from Australia or Canada, but flights via London or other European airports are not hard to arrange.

Dubrovnik's airport (Zračna Luka; www.airport-dubrovnik.hr) is at Čilipi, about 20km (12 miles) south. Platanus Travel Agency runs a bus service between the airport and the main bus station that connects with the arrival of scheduled flights (€10 one way, €15 return). The buses are very straightforward, efficient and take about 30 minutes to reach Pile Gate. Dubrovnik's Libertas bus service also goes to the airport, with tickets costing from €5.20 each way. You can take a taxi (about €35–€40), but bear in mind that the driver won't be able to drop you off anywhere inside the old town.

Arrival by road

Many drivers take on the Adriatic Highway (Jadranska Magistrala), a breathtaking route that hugs the Adriatic coast. It's also impossibly busy in summer. A more practical route is the A1 two-lane motorway that is further inland and is getting extended all the time towards Dubrovnik. There are plans to extend the four-lane E65 motorway to Dubrovnik, which should be completed by 2029. The opening in 2022 of the Pelješac bridge bypasses the need to drive briefly into Bosnia and get stuck in customs queues.

Public transport

Buses. Dubrovnik's bus service, run by Libertas (020-441 444; www.libertasdubrovnik.com), is excellent, and unless you are out very late at night is probably the only form of transport you will need in the city. The Libertas kiosks at the bus station (Autobusni Kolodvor) on Put Republike, at the city end of Gruž Harbour and at the bus stops by Pile Gate will provide you with an up-to-date timetable, as will the tourist office and most hotel reception desks. You can pay on the bus (exact money only, €2.50 at the time of writing), but it's cheaper and easier to buy tickets at newsagents' kiosks (there's usually one near main bus stops), at your hotel or on the Libertas app. For many visitors, the No.6 is the most useful route, as it runs from Pile Gate to Lapad and Babin Kuk, where many hotels are located. The service runs about six times an hour at peak periods, and continues until 1am (later in high summer).

Long-distance buses – to Zagreb, Zadar, Split and international

The small but perfectly formed harbour at Šipan

destinations – run from a bus station on Gruž Harbour (past the ferry terminal). **Boats**. There are numerous boat services to the nearby islands and to Cavtat. For boats to Cavtat and Lokrum, simply turn up at the Old Port and you will have a choice of vessels of various shapes and sizes, all charging about the same fare. For the Elaphites you can book trips through a number of different agencies, which have stands on Lapad Bay and in the Old Port. There is also a boat that shuttles across the harbour between Gruž and Lapad during the summer months.

There is a high-speed service that runs from Split to Dubrovnik, stopping at Hvar and Korčula, run by Krilo (021-645 476; www.krilo.hr). TP Line (020-313 119; www.tp-line.hr) also runs catamaran services from Dubrovnik to Dalmatian destinations including Mljet, Korčula and Lastovo. The service between Bari in Italy and Dubrovnik is run by Jadrolinja (www.jadrolinija.hr). **Taxis**. Taxi fares are metered and are not exorbitant. There are taxi stands outside Pile Gate (which lists prices to major destinations), outside Ploče Gate, at Gruž Harbour (in front of the Jadrolinija office) and by the bus station. Radio Taxi Dubrovnik runs a 24-hour service (020-411 411). Taxi meters must be running for the fare to be valid, so double check before you go very far.

Driving

Unless you are visiting Dubrovnik as part of an extended tour of Croatia, travelling by car is not a good option. Cars are not allowed into the Old Town and parking in the New Town can be difficult. However, if you do travel by car, try to find a hotel with private parking, and leave your car there when you arrive, or stay outside the town in Cavtat or Zaton and make trips in by bus or boat.

If you are driving, remember to drive on the right and stick to the speed limits of 130kph (80mph) on motorways, 100kph (62mph) on dual carriageways, 50kph (30mph) in built-up areas and 80kph (50mph) outside built-up areas, or you could risk a heavy fine. Police are also clamping down on drink-driving. **Car and scooter rental**. If you want to hire a car to make trips outside the city, you could book in advance by checking www.carrentals.co.uk, which lists the best deals from a huge number of companies.

Europcar has an office at Dubrovnik airport (098-231 079), as does Hertz (020-771 568). Gulliver (a reliable local company) is at Obala Stjepana Radića 25 (www.gulliver.hr). Avis also has an office at the airport (091 314 3019) which it shares with Budget and in town at Kardinala Stepinca 60 (095 9222 333). Brabel at Oraška 2 (www.brabel.hr) also has scooter and motorcycle rental.

Parking. There is a 24-hour car park outside the Old Town at Ilijina Glavica, and at Gruž Harbour, which at the time of writing charges €3 an hour or a daily rate of €40. The car park in Gruž is very convenient if you plan to take a ferry journey from the harbour. There are smaller car parks outside the Old Town, which are payable by parking vouchers bought at newspaper kiosks, at parking meters (exact change) and via SMS message on mobile phones.

Petrol. There's a petrol station between Gruž and the Old Town on Ulica Vladimira Nazora and another on Ulica Ante Starčevića that are both open 24hrs daily, and one on Obala Lapadska beside Lapad harbour.

Travel outside Croatia

Visiting Montenegro. Visitors to Dubrovnik have the opportunity of a day excursion to the Bay of Kotor (Boka Kotorska), which lies just over the border in Montenegro 40km (25 miles) to the south. A UNESCO World Heritage Site, the huge Bay of Kotor is a sunken river canyon, 28km (16 miles) long and 30m (100ft) deep, with four distinct bays. It is a breathtaking sight, especially for anyone arriving by boat. The bay has a number of beaches, resorts and small islands, and much of the ancient architecture in the fishing and boat-building villages is from the Venetian period.

The airport for the region is 4km (2.5 miles) outside Tivat, a largely ninettenth-century town in the southernmost bay. The naval base built by the Austrians is in private hands and has been turned into Porto Montenegro, with hundreds of berths for superyachts and the depressing ambition of becoming the Monaco of the Adriatic.

Beaches and resorts continue down the coast to the Budva Riviera (Budvanska rivijera), a playground with 11km (7 miles) of fine sandy beaches. Its beauty is at great risk of being eroded, unfortunately, as development has been racing along at dizzying speed. Construction cranes are a ubiquitous sight as foreign buyers fill every available space. Budva does have a very attractive walled old town, though, which was almost entirely rebuilt after an earthquake in 1978.

Montenegro's capital, Podgorica, is a modern, workmanlike city of around 165,000. Much of it was destroyed in World War II, but there is still an old Turkish quarter and some interesting restored churches. The city has an active cultural life, and socialising takes place out of doors in the main square, Trg Republike.

Montenegro's old royal capital is Cetinje, on the inland road between Podgorica and Kotor, and it remains the country's cultural and educational centre. Its museums and galleries provide an idea of Montenegro and its past. These include an art museum with the most valuable murals in Montenegro. Icons can also

Driving through the heartland

be seen in the Museum of Cetinje Monastery. The National Museum is housed in the palace of Nikola I Petrović-Njegoš, Montenegro's only king, who reigned 1910–18.

A fast passenger ferry run by Adriatic Lines (www.adriatic-lines.com) goes between Dubrovnik and Budva from June to September four to seven times a week, and from Dubrovnik to Kotor three times a week. Trips can be made independently if you hire a car, which is easy to take into Montenegro. Tour companies such as Viator (www.viator.com) organise day trips that usually include Kotor, Cetinje and Budva. There are buses that go to the main towns in Montenegro, but their schedules don't leave much flexibility if you want to see more than one place in a day.

Villa/apartment rentals

Numerous companies offer rentals in villas and apartments to suit most budgets, ranging from small flats in the Old Town to large villas in the surrounding countryside. Here is a selection:
Croatian Villa Holidays: www.croatianvillaholidays.com.
Croatian Villas: www.croatianvillas.com.
Croatia Gems: www.croatiagems.com.
Completely Croatia: www.completelycroatia.co.uk.
Oliver's Travels: www.oliverstravels.com.
Vintage Travel: www.vintagetravel.co.uk.

Rose of Dubrovnik: www.dubrovnikapartmentsvillas.com.

Visas and passports

Citizens of EU countries, and those from the UK, Australia, New Zealand, the US and Canada, need only a valid passport to visit Croatia for stays of up to three months. If you are going on day trips to Bosnia-Herzegovina or Montenegro you need to take your passport with you, but you don't need a visa.

All foreign visitors are required to register with the police within 24 hours of their arrival, but in practice this is done by the hotel or owner of the private accommodation in which you are staying, and it is their responsibility, not yours, to see that it is done.

Weights and measures

Croatia uses the metric system.

Websites

Useful websites include:
www.tzdubrovnik.hr; www.croatia.hr; www.frankaboutcroatia.com; www.buscroatia.com; www.visit-croatia.co.uk

Women travellers

Female travellers do not usually experience harassment in Dubrovnik, and anyone making unwanted advances will generally take a firm no for an answer. However, taking the usual precautions is sensible, such as avoiding walking alone at night.

Mljet lake scene

Language

Croatian is a difficult language for non-native speakers to grasp; it's an inflected language with seven cases, three genders and a complicated set of grammar rules. And the Dalmatian dialect often creeps into conversation, which can cause extra confusion. Although most people in the tourism industry in Dubrovnik speak English very well, a few words of Croatian are appreciated by locals in the rural regions.

Pronunciation tips

Croatians use a customised version of the Roman alphabet, with the pronunciation of many letters being the same in Croatian and English. Every single letter is pronounced and their sounds do not change from word to word.

The stress never falls on the last syllable.

c like the 'ts' in 'hats'
ć like the 'tu' in 'nature'
č like the 'ch' in 'chip'
đ like the 'du' in 'endure' (sometimes written dj if the correct character is unavailable)
dž like the 'j' in 'juice'
j like the 'y' in 'yacht'
lj like the 'lli' in 'billion'
nj like the 'ny' in 'banyan'
š like the 'sh' in 'lush'
ž like the 's' in 'treasure'

Useful phrases

Hello. *Bok.*
Good morning. *Dobro jutro.*
Good day/afternoon. *Dobar dan.*
Good evening. *Dobra večer.*
Good night. *Laku noć.*
Goodbye. *Do viđenja.*
Welcome. *Dobro došli.*
My name is … *Moje ime je …*
How are you? *Kako ste?*
Yes *Da*
No *Ne*
Where? When? How? *Gdje? Kada? Kako?*
How much? *Koliko?*
Thank you. *Hvala.*
Please *Molim*
Excuse me, please. *Oprostite, molim.*
Do you speak (English, German, Italian, Croatian)? *Govorite li (engleski, njemački, talijanski, hrvatski)?*
I (don't) speak *(Ne) govorim*
I (don't) understand *(Ne) razumijem*
Cheers *Živjeli*

Somewhere to stay

Can you recommend…? *Možete li preporučiti…?*
a hotel *hotel*
a hostel *hostel*
a campsite *kamp*
a bed and breakfast *polupansion*
What is it near? *Što se nalazi u blizini?*
How do I get there? *Kako mogu stići tamo?*

Most restaurants in Dubrovnik will have menus in English

At the hotel

Do you have …? *Imate li… ?*
a room *sobu*
a single room *jednokrevetnu sobu*
a double room *dvokrevetnu sobu*
with a shower/bath *sa tušem/banjom*
one night/week *jednu noć/tjedan*
Bed and breakfast *noćenje i doručak*
Full board/half board *pansion/polupansion*
How much is it …? *Koliko košta za …?*
per night *jednu noć*
per person *po osobi*
balcony *balkon*
terrace *terasa*
Is there anything cheaper? *Ima li nešto jeftinije?*
When's check-out? *Kada moramo napustiti?*
Can I leave this in the safe? *Mogu li ostaviti ovo u sefu?*
Can I leave my bags? *Mogu li ostaviti torbe?*
Can I have my bill/a receipt? *Mogu li dobiti račun/priznanicu?*
I'll pay in cash/by credit card. *Plaćam gotovinom/kreditnom karticom.*

At the bar/restaurant

Restaurant *restoran*
Breakfast *doručak*
Lunch *ručak*
Coffee house *kavana*
Drink *piće*
One portion *jednu porciju*
Have you got a table for …? *Imate li stol za … osobe?*
May I have the menu (wine list)? *Molim vas jelovnik (vinsku kartu)?*
Have you got any food for vegetarians? *Imate li nešto za vegetarijance?*
Thank you, it was delicious *Bilo je jako dobro*
The bill, please *Račun molim*
Beer *pivo*
Black coffee *crna kava*
Brandy *rakija*
Fruit juice *voćni sok*
Mineral water *mineralna voda*
Plum brandy *šljivovica*
Table wine *stolno vino* (**also seen on menus as** *otvoreno vino* – "open wine")
Tea *čaj*
with milk/lemon, rum *s mlijekom/s limunom/s rumom*
Wine (white, red, rosé) *vino (bijelo, crno, roze)*
Bread *kruh*
Cheese *sir*
Cold meat *hladno pečenje*
Ham (raw, cooked, smoked) *šunka (sirova, kuhana, dimljena)*
Olives *masline*
Soup *juha*
Beefsteak *biftek*
Chicken *pile*
Pork chops *svinjski kotleti*
Lamb on the spit *janje na ražnju*
Turkey *tuka*
Veal cutlet *teleći odrezak*
Cucumber *krastavac*
Green pepper *paprika*
Mushrooms *gljive*

Street sign

POD TVRĐAVOM

Onion *luk*
Potato *krumpir*
Salad *salata*
Cake *kolač*
Fruit salad *voćna salata*
Ice cream *sladoled*
Pancakes *palačinke*

Numbers

0 *nula*
1 *jedan*
2 *dva*
3 *tri*
4 *četiri*
5 *pet*
6 *šest*
7 *sedam*
8 *osam*
9 *devet*
10 *deset*
11 *jedanaest*
12 *dvanaest*
20 *dvadeset*
30 *trideset*
40 *četrdeset*
50 *pedeset*
60 *šezdeset*
70 *sedamdeset*
80 *osamdeset*
90 *devedeset*
100 *sto*
1,000 *tisuću*

Public transport and getting around

Where is the …? *Gdje je …?*
railway station? *željeznička postaja?*
bus stop? *autobusna postaja?*

What time does the … leave? *U koliko sati polazi …?*
train/bus/ferry? *vlak/autobus/trajekt?*
one way ticket *jednosmjerna/karta*
return ticket *povratna karta*
Booking *rezervacija*
Airport *zračna luka*
Timetable *raspored*
How much is the ticket to …? *Koliko košta karta za …?*

Shopping

Do you have …? *Imate li …?*
How much is it …? *Kolika košta …?*
Bakery *pekara/pekarnica*
Butchers *mesnica*
Department store *robna kuća*
Grocer *dućan*
Laundry *praonica rublja*
Market *tržnica*
Pastry shop *slastičarnica*
Supermarket *samoposluživanje*
Price *cijena*
Cheap *jeftino*
Expensive *skupo*

Money

Where's…? *Gdje je…?*
the ATM *bankomat*
the bank *banka*
the currency exchange office *mjenjačnica*
What time does the bank open/close? *Kada se banka otvara/zatvara?*
I'd like to change some dollars/pounds into euros. *Htio m/Htjela f bih promijeniti dolare/funte u eure.*

Konoba sign

Telephone

I would like to buy a phone card/prepaid phone, please. *Htio bih kupiti telefonsku karticu/ Prepaid telefon, molim Vas.*
How much? *Koliko*
Can I recharge/buy minutes for this phone? *Mogu li napuniti/kupiti nadoplatni bon za ovaj telefon?*
Where's the pay phone? *Gdje je telefonska govornica?*
What's the area/country code for…? *Koji je regionalni/ državni pozivni broj za…?*
What's the number for information, please? *Koji je broj informacija, molim Vas?*
I'd like the number for… *Htio m/Htjela f bih broj za…*
I'd like to call collect [reverse the charges]. *Htio m/Htjela f bih nazvati na račun primatelja poziva.*
My phone doesn't work here. *Moj telefon ne radi ovdje.*
What network are you on? *Na kojoj si mreži?*
Is it 5G? *Je li to 5G?*
Do you have a phone charger I could borrow? *Imate li punjač za mobitel mogao bih posuditi?*
Can I have your number? *Mogu li dobiti vaš broj?*
Here's my number. *To je moj broj.*
Please call/text me. *Molim vas nazovite me/napišite mi poruku.*
I'll call you. *Nazvat ću vas*
I will send you a text. *Napisat ću vam poruku.*

Online access and communication

Where's an internet café? *Gdje ima internet cafe?*
Does it have wireless internet? *Ima li bežični internet?*
What is the Wi-Fi password? *Koja je lozinka za bežičnu mrežu?*
Is the Wi-Fi free? *Je li bežična mreža besplatna?*
What's your email address? *Koja je vaša e-mail adresa?*
My email address is… *Moja e-mail adresa je…*
Can I…? *Mogu li…?*
use any computer *koristiti bilo koji računar*
access the internet *pristupiti internetu*
check my email *provjeriti e-mail*
print *printati*
plug in/charge my laptop/ iPhone/iPad? *uključiti/napuniti svoj laptop/iPhone/iPad?*
access Skype? *Mogu li koristiti Skype?*

Social media

Are you on Facebook/Instagram? *Jesi li na Facebooku/Instagramu?*
What's your username? *Koje ti je korisničko ime?*
I will add you as a friend on Facebook. *Dodat ću te za prijatelja na Facebooku.*
I'll follow you on Instagram. *Slijedit ću te na Instagramu.*
I'll put the pictures on Facebook/Instagram. *Stavit ću slike na Facebook/Instagram.*

Mushrooms for sale

Cocktail Bar Massimo

Books and film

Dubrovnik received an unexpected boost in 2010 when the city became the setting for the HBO television series *Game of Thrones*, subsequently attracting a new generation of visitors. But the history of Dubrovnik is more dramatic than anything that the HBO producers can dream up. And because the events of the 1990s Homeland War are often baffling to visitors, some background reading can help to put the city's modern history into context.

Books

History

The National Question in Yugoslavia by Ivo Banac. An examination of the tension between Serbian nationalism, Croatian nationalism and Yugoslavianism in the Balkans from the mid-nineteenth century to the 1921 Vidovdan Constitution.

The Yugoslav Auschwitz and the Vatican: The Croatian Massacre of the Serbs During World War II by Vladimir Dedijer. Written by a former Yugoslav ambassador to the UN, this well-researched book covers an episode of history that many Croatians – and Roman Catholics – would prefer had remained secret.

The Balkans 1804–1999: Nationalism, War and the Great Powers by Misha Glenny. An ambitious attempt to explain the history of the Balkans and how the rest of the world meddled in its affairs.

Croatia: A History by Ivo Goldstein. An unbiased, authoritative history of the country written by a professor at Zagreb University.

The Impossible Country: A Journey Through the Last Days of Yugoslavia by Brian Hall. An engrossing account of the author's journey during the last days of Yugoslavia in 1991.

Dubrovnik: A History by Robin Harris. A detailed, weighty, but accessible history of the city.

Balkan Ghosts: A Journey Through History by Robert D Kaplan. A brilliant take on the 20th-century history of the Balkans by an American war reporter.

Croatia Through History by Branka Magaš. Despite being Croatian, historian and journalist Branka Magaš bravely attempts to cover objectively the history of Croatia from the Middle Ages to the present and does it remarkably well.

The Demise of Yugoslavia: A Political Memoir by Stjepan Mesić. Insightful account of the collapse of the former Yugoslavia written by the federation's last president, and the first democratically elected president of the independent Croatian state.

The Death of Yugoslavia by Laura Silber and Alan Little. A riveting account of the events that contributed

Game of Thrones tourism is big business in Dubrovnik

to the 1991 war and running on to the Dayton Accord, presented from a historical perspective.
How We Survived Communism and Even Laughed by Slavenka Drakulić. A collection of essays that examine life under Communism.
Balkan Express by Slavenka Drakulić. An exploration of the effects of the Homeland War on the lives of ordinary people.
Croatia: A Nation Forged in War by Marcus Tanner. A compelling account of Croatian history, from the Greeks and Romans to the present day.

Gastronomy
A Taste of Croatia: Savoring the Food, People and Traditions of Croatia's Adriatic Coast by Karen Evenden. Not so much a cookbook as a love letter celebrating its subject.
My Favourite Croatian Recipes by Sandra Lougher. One of few books about Croatian food in English.
The Best of Croatian Cooking – Expanded Edition by Liliana Pavičić and Gordana Pirker-Mosher. As well as 200 recipes, the book covers Croatia's culinary tradition and local specialities.

Travel
Chasing a Croatian Girl by Cody Brown. A witty tale of an American professor at Zagreb University who falls in love with a Croatian girl, a relationship that becomes a window into Croatia's culture and people.
Croatia: Travels in Undiscovered Country by Tony Fabijančić. A travelogue written by a Canadian-born son of Croatian immigrants exploring his ancestral homeland.
Black Lamb and Grey Falcon by Rebecca West. West's colossal account of several journeys through Yugoslavia during the 1930s is essential reading for an understanding of Balkan history.

Fiction
Croatian Nights ed. Borivoj Radaković, Matt Thorne and Tony White. Eclectic collection of short stories by Croatian and British writers, which grew out of the Festival of Alternative Literature.
The Museum of Unconditional Surrender by Dubravka Ugrešić. A novel that weaves humour and bitterness honing in on the life of a 45-year-old Croatian woman living in exile.

Television and film
Cure: The Life of Another (2014) Dubrovnik just after the 1991–92 siege is the setting for this unsettling thriller about two teenage girls.
Game of Thrones HBO's incredibly popular fantasy drama set in the Middle Ages have been filmed in Dubrovnik.
Penelope (2009) Filmed in Dubrovnik, this Croatian-Australian co-production takes the woman's point of view in Homer's *Odyssey*, as long-suffering Penelope waits for her husband Odysseus to return.

On set: Dubrovnik starred in *Game of Thrones*

About this book

The Rough Guides Walks & Tours series helps you discover the world's most exciting destinations through our expert-curated trip plans: a range of walks and tours designed to suit all budgets, interests and trip lengths. These walks, driving tours and site excursions cover the destination's most quintessential attractions as well as a range of lesser-known sights, while food and drink stops for refreshments en route are highlighted in boxes. If you're not sure which walk to pick, our Best walks & tours for… feature suggests which ones work best for particular interests. The introduction provides a destination overview, while the directory supports the walks and tours with all the essential information you need, as well as our pick of where to stay while you are there and select restaurant listings, to complement the more low-key options given in the trip plans.

About the authors

Rough Guides Walks & Tours Dubrovnik was written and researched by Mary Novakovich, an award-winning journalist and travel writer based in Hertfordshire. She has been visiting Croatia, where her parents were born, since the 1970s and goes back frequently. She contributes regularly to *The Times*, *The Guardian*, *The Independent* and *The Telegraph*, and is also the author of *My Family and Other Enemies: Life and Travels in Croatia's Hinterland*, which won the 2023 British Guild of Travel Writers' Best Travel Narrative Book and was also shortlisted for the Edward Stanford Travel Book of the Year 2023.

Help us update

We've gone to a lot of effort to ensure that this edition of the **Rough Guides Walks & Tours Dubrovnik** is accurate and up-to-date. However, things change – places get "discovered", new gems open up, restaurants and rooms raise prices or lower standards. If you feel we've got it wrong or left something out, we'd like to know, and if you can remember the address, the website, whether or not it was free to enter – so much the better.

Please send your comments with the subject line "**Rough Guides Walks & Tours Dubrovnik Update**" to mail@uk.roughguides.com. We'll acknowledge all contributions and send a copy of the next edition (or any other Rough Guide if you prefer) for the very best emails.

Credits

Rough Guides Walks & Tours Dubrovnik
Editor: Lizzie Horrocks
Author: Mary Novakovich
Picture Editor: Piotr Kala
Picture Manager: Tom Smyth
Cartography: Katie Bennett
Layout: Grzegorz Madejak
Production Operations Manager: Katie Bennett
Publishing Technology Manager: Rebeka Davies
Head of Publishing: Sarah Clark
Photo credits: All images Shutterstock except: Bigstock 18; Borko Vukosav 100/101; Corrie Wingate/Apa Publications 4BR, 6BC, 16, 16/17, 17R, 19, 21, 24, 26, 80, 81R, 82, 83, 101R, 118, 118/119, 119R; Dominic Burdon/APA Publications 6TL, 7T, 7MR, 14, 30, 32, 33R, 32/33, 38, 39R, 43, 66, 67, 78, 79, 80/81, 98, 100, 106, 107, 109, 114; Esculap Restaurants 96, 96/97, 97R; Goran Ergović/Croatian Tourist Board 25R; Hotel Stari Grad 86, 87, 94, 95; iStock 1, 38/39, 46, 58/59, 60, 68, 68/69, 69R, 72/73, 108, 110, 111, 117; iStockphoto 52; Leonardo 51, 88, 88/89, 89R
Cover credits: Dubrovnik iStock

Printed by Finidr in Czech Republic

This book was produced using **Typefi** automated publishing software.

A catalogue record for this book is available from the British Library.

All Rights Reserved
© 2025 Apa Digital AG
License edition © Apa Publications Ltd UK

First Edition 2025

ISBN: 9781835292617

MIX
Paper from responsible sources
FSC® C014138

No part of this book may be reproduced, stored in a retrieval system or transmitted in any form or means electronic, mechanical, photocopying, recording or otherwise, without prior written permission from Apa Publications.

Every effort has been made to ensure that this publication is accurate, free from safety risks, and provides accurate information. However, changes and errors are inevitable. The publisher is not responsible for any resulting loss, inconvenience, injury or safety concerns arising from the use of this book.

Distribution

UK, Ireland and Europe
Apa Publications (UK) Ltd; mail@roughguides.com
United States and Canada
Two Rivers; ips@ingramcontent.com
Australia and New Zealand
Woodslane; info@woodslane.com.au
Worldwide
Apa Publications (UK) Ltd; mail@roughguides.com

Special Sales, Content Licensing and CoPublishing

Rough Guides can be purchased in bulk quantities at discounted prices. We can create special editions, personalized jackets and corporate imprints tailored to your needs.
mail@roughguides.com
http://roughguides.com

EU Representative

LOGOS EUROPE, 9 rue Nicolas Poussin, 17000, LA ROCHELLE, France
Contact@logoseurope.eu; +33 (0) 667937378

Index

A
accessible travel 106
age restrictions 106

B
Babin Kuk peninsula 53
Badija 83
Banje Beach 50
bars 104
Bokar Fortress 30
budgeting 106

C
cable car 52
casinos 105
Cathedral 40
Cavtat 71
    Baltazar Bogišić Collection 72
    Bukovac House 74
    Franciscan Monastery Church 72
    Konavle County Museum 74
    Račić Family Mausoleum 73
    St Nicholas 72
children 106
Church of Sveti Vlaho 39
cinema 105
climate 12
clothing 107
clubs 105
concert venues 104
Copacabana Beach 56
crime and safety 107
customs 107

D
Dominican Church and Monastery 43
Donje Čelo 62
Dulčić, Masle, Pulitika Gallery 33, 41

E
electricity 107
embassies and consulates 107
emergency numbers 107
entertainment 22
etiquette 108

F
festivals 23, 108
food and drink 16
Fort Lovrijenac 34
Franciscan Convent and Church of Danče 34
Franciscan Monastery 30
Franciscan Monastery and Museum 36
Franjo Tuđman Bridge 61

G
Game of Thrones 34, 76
geography 10
Gornje Čelo 62
Gradac 35
Gradska Vijećnica 39
Gruž 57
Gundulićeva Poljana (Gundulić Square) 41

H
health 108
history 11, 26
Home of Marin Držić 47
hospitals 108
Hotel Belvedere 52
hotels
    Aminess Korčula Heritage 93
    Bellevue 89
    Bokun Guesthouse 89
    Boutique and Beach Hotel 89
    Božica 92
    Casa Bianca 88
    Castelleto 92
    Croatia 92
    Dubrovnik Palace 89
    Excelsior 88
    Glanović 93
    Heritage Hotel Nobile 88
    Hilton Imperial 88
    Karmen Apartments 86
    Kazbek 89
    Komodor 90
    Kompas 90
    L'Amoret Apartments 86
    Lapad 90
    Lero 89
    Lešić Dimitri Palace 93
    More 90
    Odisej 93
    PineTree Boutique Apartments 93
    President 91
    Prijeko Palace 87
    Pucić Palace 87
    Remisens Hotel Albatros 92
    Rixos Premium Dubrovnik 89
    RMH Lopud Lafodia 93
    Royal Hotels & Resort 91
    Scalini Palace 87
    Splendid 90
    Stari Grad 87
    St Joseph's 87
    Sun Gardens Dubrovnik 91
    Supetar 92
    The Byron 86
    TUI BLUE Kalamota Island Resort 92
    Uvala 90
    Valamar Argosy 91
    Valamar Tirena 91
    Vila Koruna 93
    Vila Mičika 90
    Villa Dubrovnik 88
    Villa Odak 88
    Villa Orsula 88
    Villa Pattiera 92
    Villa Ragusa 87
    Vis 90
hours and holidays 109

I
Icon Museum 48
internet facilities 109

J
Jesuit Church 46

K
Koločep 62
Korčula 79
    All Saints' Church 82

Gradska Vijećnica 83
Icon Museum 82
Kopnena Vrata 83
Marco Polo Tower 82
Primorska Vrata 80
St Mark's Cathedral 80
Town Museum 81
Treasury Museum 81
Velika Kneževa Kula 83
Veliko Revelin 83

L
language 116
Lapad 53
    Uvala Lapad 53
Lazareti 49
LGBTQ+ travellers 109
Lokrum 58
    Botanical Gardens 59
    forest of holm oak 60
    Fort Royal 60
    monastery 59
    Mrtvo More 59
    Portoč 59
Lopud 63
    Plaža Šunj 65
    port 64
    St Mary of Spilica church 64
Lumbarda 83
Luža Square 37

M
Marin Držič Theatre 39
Maritime Museum 31
media 109
Memorial Room of Dubrovnik
    Defenders 38
Minčeta Fortress 34
Mljet 66
    Babine Kuće 69
    Babino Polje 69
    Limuni Beach 70
    Malo Jezero 67
    Mljet National Park 66
    Polače 66
    Pomena 68
    Pristanište 67
    Saplunara 70
    Sobra 69
    Sutmiholjska 70
    Sveta Marija 67
    Veliko Jezero 67
money 109
Museum of Modern Art 50
Museum of the Homeland War 52

N
nightlife 22, 104

O
Old Port 39
Orlando's Column 37
Orsan Yacht Club 57
outdoor activities 24

P
Pile Gate 30
Ploče Gate 49
post 110
post office 53

R
Rector's Palace 39
Red History Museum 57
religion 110
restaurants
    7 Seas Restaurant and Bar 103
    360° 95
    Above 5 Rooftop Restaurant 95
    Azur 95
    Barba 95
    Bistro Revelin 98
    Bistro Tavulin 98
    Bota Šare Oyster & Sushi
        Bar 95
    Bota Šare Restaurant & Oyster
        Bar 103
    Bougenvila 101
    BOWA 101
    Bura Bistro and Bar 96
    Dalmacija 102
    Dalmatino 96
    Dubravka 1836 Restaurant &
        Café 98
    Dubrovnik Beer Company 99
    Eden Kitchen & Bar 100
    Ezza Steak & Cocktail Bar
        98
    Fish & Seafood Restaurant
        Casa 100
    Gusta Me 98
    Kamenice 96
    Konoba Aquarius 96
    Konoba Feral 103
    Konoba Galicija 102
    Konoba Herc 102
    Konoba Ivan 102
    Konoba Kenova 98
    Konoba Mandrač 101
    Konoba Peggy 101
    Konoba-Pizzeria Blidinje 99
    Lady PiPi 96
    LD Restaurant 103
    Levanat 100
    Lucin Kantun 96
    Mea Culpa 96
    Nautika 98
    Nishta 96
    Panorama 99
    Pizzeria Oliva 97
    Porat Restaurant 99
    Posat 98
    Proto 97
    Restaurant Dubrovnik 97
    Restaurant Filippi 103
    Restaurant Komin 100
    Restaurant Magdalena 97
    Restaurant Obala 101
    Restaurant Orsan 100
    Restaurant Pantarul 100
    Restaurant Zoë 100
    Restoran Stermasi 102
    Rozario 97
    Sesame 99
    Shizuku Japanese Cuisine
        101
    Spaghetteria Toni 97
    Stara Loza 97
    Stella Maris 102
    Taj Mahal 97
    Urban & Veggie Vegan Restaurant
        100
    Villa Koruna 103
    Villa Ruža 101
    Zino 102
Revelin Fortress 49
Rupe Ethnographic Museum 47

S

Sebastian Gallery 43
shopping 20
Šipan 62
Šipanska Luka 63
Skoji islands 83
smoking 110
Sponza Palace 38
Ston 77
    oysters 78
Stradun 36
Suđurad 63
Sveta Margarita 31
Sveti Jakova 33
Sveti Spasitelj Fortress 31
Sveti Stjepan 31
Synagogue and Museum 45

T

telephones 110
theatre 105
time zones 111
toilets 111
tourist information 111
tours and guides 111
transport 111
Trsteno 76
    Arboretum 76

V

villa/apartment rentals 115
Villa Scheherazade 51
visas and passports 115
Visiting Montenegro 114

W

War Photo Limited 45
websites 115
weights and measures 115
women travellers 115

Z

Zaton 75

MAP LEGEND

- ● Start of tour
- → Tour & route direction
- ❶ Recommended sight
- ❶ Recommended restaurant/café
- ★ Place of interest
- ❶ Tourist information
- 1 Statue/monument
- ✉ Main post office
- 🚌 Main bus station
- ☼ Viewpoint
- Park
- Important building
- Hotel
- Transport hub
- Market/store
- Pedestrian area
- Urban area

NOTES